W9-BZW-696

A Beginner's Guide to BASIC

Charles S. Parker

The College of Santa Fe
Santa Fe, New Mexico

The Dryden Press
A Harcourt Brace Jovanovich College Publisher
Fort Worth   Philadelphia   San Diego
New York   Orlando   Austin   San Antonio
Toronto   Montreal   London   Sydney   Tokyo

Acquisitions Editor: DeVilla Williams
Developmental Editor: Rita West
Project Editor: Karen Hill
Art and Design Manager: Alan Wendt
Production Manager: Barb Bahnsen
Permissions Editor: Doris Milligan
Director of Editing, Design, and Production: Jane Perkins

Copy Editor: Judy Lary
Compositor: The Clarinda Company
Text Type: 9/11 Palatino

Library of Congress Cataloging-in-Publication Data

Parker, Charles S., 1945–
    A beginner's guide to BASIC / Charles S. Parker.
        p.   cm.
    Also published as an appendix to the author's Understanding
computers and information processing.
    ISBN 0-03-074451-2
   1. BASIC (Computer program language)   I. Title.
QA76.73.B3P254   1991
005.265—dc20   91-19802

Printed in the United States of America
123-066-987654321
Copyright © 1992 by The Dryden Press.

All rights reserved. No part of this publication may be reproduced or transmitted in any form or by any means, electronic or mechanical, including photocopy, recording, or any information storage and retrieval system, without permission in writing from the publisher.

Some material in this work previously appeared in *Understanding Computers and Information Processing: Today and Tomorrow,* Third Edition, copyright © 1990, 1987, 1984 by The Dryden Press. All rights reserved.

Requests for permission to make copies of any part of the work should be mailed to: Permission Department, Harcourt Brace Jovanovich, Publishers, 8th Floor, Orlando, FL 32887.

Address orders:
The Dryden Press
Orlando, Florida 32887

Address editorial correspondence:
The Dryden Press
301 Commerce Street, Suite 3700
Forth Worth, TX 76102

The Dryden Press
Harcourt Brace Jovanovich

Cover Source: Copyright © 1991 James Dowlen.

A Beginner's Guide to BASIC

BASIC (Beginner's All-purpose Symbolic Instruction Code) is one of many programming languages in use today. A programming language is a set of rules used to create a computer program. The computer program is what you enter into the computer system to produce results.

A BASIC computer program is very similar to a recipe. It consists of a list of instructions the computer must carry out in a specified sequence to produce the desired result. Each of the instructions in a BASIC program must be written in strict accordance with the rules of the BASIC language. These rules are referred to as syntax. If you make a seemingly trivial syntax error in writing the program, such as misspelling a word or omitting a comma, the computer system will reject your program or give unexpected, incorrect results.

The purpose of this Guide is to teach you how to write useful, simple BASIC programs. Of all the major programming languages, BASIC is among the easiest to learn. You should be able to create programs for business use, game playing, and performing difficult, repetitive computations after reading this Guide and practicing on a computer.

Many versions of the BASIC language are available today. A Beginner's Guide to BASIC has been written to conform to one of the most common BASIC usages, BASICA and similar versions of BASIC on microcomputer systems that use either the MS-DOS or PC-DOS operating systems. In the pages that follow, program outputs are distinguished from programs and their inputs by highlighting in color.

The need to practice BASIC on a computer can't be emphasized enough. Programming, like driving a car or playing a sport, is a skill that is mastered mostly by practice. Since it is easy for a beginner in any endeavor to make mistakes at the beginning, practicing can initially be very frustrating (can you remember your first day with a musical instrument?). However, if you really want to learn BASIC, and if you start by writing simple programs rather than complicated ones, you will find BASIC to be relatively easy. So, be patient—and start playing with your computer as soon as possible.

Here's what's on the following pages.

SECTION 1
A BASIC PRIMER

A Simple Example

Let's get into BASIC immediately by looking at a relatively simple problem and developing a BASIC program to solve it. The example given in Figure 1-1 will show you both some of the rules of BASIC and the manner in which computers carry out instructions in a logical, step-by-step fashion.

The problem is to write a BASIC program that adds the numbers 8 and 16. We want the computer to print the answer like this:

```
THE ANSWER IS 24
```

There are many ways to solve this problem, including the one shown in Figure 1-1.

The six numbered instructions in the figure make up a *BASIC program.* In most cases, you will be typing in instructions such as these at a keyboard hooked up to a computer. When you have finished typing in and entering the instructions (pressing the Enter key after each instruction), you then normally type the word RUN to command the system to execute (that is, to carry out) your program. You should study this program carefully before proceeding further. Sometimes the purpose of an instruction will be obvious. The comments that follow shortly should clarify the other instructions.

Before we go into detail about precisely how the program works, you should observe the following important points about the program in Figure 1-1:

1. Each of the six numbered instructions is a *BASIC program statement.* The computer completes the operation described in each statement. It then automatically moves on to another statement.

    Each BASIC program statement begins with a key word that tells the computer what type of operation is involved—for example, REM, READ, LET, PRINT, DATA, and END. These key words may be thought of as the vocabulary of the computer system when you are writing BASIC programs. You must always stay strictly within this vocabulary. If, for example, you substitute DATUM or DATTA for DATA in line 50, the computer system will not know what you want to do.

2. Each program statement is identified by a *line number*—for example, 10, 20, 30, and so on. Line numbers are normally written in increments of 10 rather than 1, which makes it easy to insert new statements in the program later. All line numbers must be integers (whole numbers), and all lines must have different line numbers.

    The computer will always execute statements in the sequence specified by the line numbers unless instructed to do otherwise. Ways to do this are discussed later in this section. Because the line numbers specify the order of program statements, you can type in the lines in any order, such as 30, 60, 10, 50, 20, and 40. Before the computer system runs your program, it will automatically put all the statements in proper order by line number.

Figure 1-1
A simple BASIC program.

```
10 REM THIS PROGRAM ADDS TWO NUMBERS
20 READ NUMBER1, NUMBER2
30 LET SUM = NUMBER1 + NUMBER2
40 PRINT "THE ANSWER IS ";SUM
50 DATA 8,16
60 END
```
⎫
⎬ BASIC program
⎭

```
RUN ◄──────────────────
THE ANSWER IS    24 ◄
```
⎰ Command instructing computer
⎱ to "execute" program

↳ Program output

---

3. In this program, three *variables* (NUMBER1, NUMBER2, and SUM) are used. When the computer system begins to execute the program, it will set up separate storage locations for each variable. A storage location can be thought of as a "bucket" that can hold only one item (for example, a number) at a time.

    The storage locations represent the memory of the computer with respect to the program being run. For example, when we ask the computer in line 40 to print the value of SUM, the computer consults its memory to find the value.

    It is possible, as we will see in later programs, to change the values of variables such as NUMBER1, NUMBER2, and SUM several times during the execution of a program. It is because their values are allowed to change that they are known as variables. When NUMBER1, NUMBER2, and SUM are given new values, their old values are lost.

Now let's see, statement by statement, how the program works.

```
10 REM THIS PROGRAM ADDS TWO NUMBERS
```

The REM (remark) statement is actually ignored by the computer. However, even though the computer doesn't use it, the REM statement is very helpful. It allows you to place informative comments (such as the program title or description) in the body of the program.

```
20 READ NUMBER1, NUMBER2    and    50 DATA 8,16
```

The READ and DATA statements are always used together in BASIC. The READ statement instructs the computer to assign data to the specified variables. The DATA statement provides these data. Note that the computer assigns values one at a time and in the order in which they are typed in the READ and DATA statements. Thus, when the READ statement is executed, the computer sets NUMBER1 equal to 8 and NUMBER2 equal to 16.

```
30 LET SUM = NUMBER1 + NUMBER2
```

The computer system always reacts to a LET statement by computing the value indicated by the expression on the right side of the "=" sign and assigning it to the variable named on the left side. Thus, statement 30 will cause the following actions to be taken:

1. The computer system looks up the values of NUMBER1 and NUMBER2 in memory (finding 8 and 16, respectively).

2. The values of NUMBER1 and NUMBER2 are added (producing 24).
3. The value of the right side of the expression (24) is assigned to SUM.

```
40 PRINT "THE ANSWER IS ";SUM
```

The PRINT statement is used when we want the computer system to output something—for example, the results of a computation. The preceding PRINT statement consists of three elements:

1. A phrase appearing inside quotes (THE ANSWER IS). The computer system will print this phrase exactly as it appears. These *literal* phrases are handy in PRINT statements to label output.
2. A formatting character (;). The semicolon instructs the computer system to leave only one space between the literal phrase and the value of SUM.
3. A variable (SUM). The computer system will look up the value of SUM in memory and print its value.

If you are using a display device, PRINT instructs the computer to display results on the screen. You must use the command LPRINT in your program if you wish to direct output to your printer instead.

```
60 END
```

On many computer systems, the END statement physically must be the last statement in the program. It instructs the computer system that the program is finished.

At this point, you can start to see how BASIC works. Now is a good time to test your knowledge of some of the fundamental concepts just introduced by practicing on your computer system. The section that follows describes how to get started with BASIC on the particular computer system you are using.

Getting Started

To begin, your computer must be turned on and you must load, or "boot up," the operating system (either MS-DOS or PC-DOS).

Dual-Diskette Systems.　On a dual-diskette system, put the diskette containing the operating system in the A drive—that is, the leftmost or topmost disk drive—and turn on the power switch. Also turn on your monitor and printer.

When the date and time prompts appear, either enter a date and time where appropriate or press the Enter key to indicate that you wish to bypass the date and time settings. If it was 7:24 P.M. on December 15, 1991, for instance, you could enter the date and time in the form 12-15-91 and 19:24, respectively.

When the A> prompt is displayed, indicating that the operating system has been successfully loaded, or booted, replace the operating system disk with the disk containing BASIC* and type

```
                    BASICA
```

Follow this by hitting the Enter key. At this point, the BASIC language translator will be loaded into primary memory, or RAM. You will see the prompting mes-

---

*The BASIC language translator is often on the same diskette that contains the operating system, stored in a file called BASICA.COM. If there is a different version of BASIC on your system, you can generally load it by typing in its main filename; for instance, type in GWBASIC if the file is named GWBASIC.EXE.

sage "Ok" on your screen, indicating that BASICA is ready for your first BASIC command.

Once BASICA is in primary memory, you no longer need to have the disk containing BASIC mounted on any of the disk drives as you use BASIC. The operating system will save programs to and retrieve programs from the default drive, A, unless you specify another disk drive in the file name. You will see how to name files a bit later.

Hard-Disk Systems.   On a hard-disk system, the date and time prompts will often be displayed as soon as you turn on your computer system. At this point, follow the same instructions as dual-diskette users for responding to both the date and time prompts. Then, when the C> prompt is displayed, type in and enter BASICA. This will load the BASIC language translator into primary memory, or RAM. You will see the prompting message "Ok" on your screen, indicating that BASICA is ready for your first BASIC command. The operating system will save programs to and retrieve programs from the C drive unless you specify another disk drive in the file name. You will see how to name files a bit later.

Entering and Editing Programs

As you type in each line of your program, don't forget to enter the line by pressing the Enter key. It is only when you press Enter that the line is actually recorded in computer memory.

If you make a mistake as you are typing in a line, you can use either the Backspace or Delete keys to delete unwanted characters or the Insert key to insert new characters. Backspace deletes the character to the left of the cursor position, whereas Delete erases the character at the cursor position. Insert is a toggle key. Pressing it once makes insertion active (note that the cursor increases in size), and pressing Insert at any time when insertion is active makes insertion inactive.

You can use the arrow keys to move to any position in the line. BASIC has a full screen editor, meaning you can make a change to any line that appears on the screen and then enter the change by pressing the Enter key. The Enter key can be pressed with the screen cursor anywhere on the line. A more comprehensive list of useful BASIC keys is provided in Figure 1-2.

As you are entering lines of a program and making edits, it is usually important to ascertain exactly what BASIC is storing in memory. To get a listing of all lines of your program on the display screen, in ascending order by line number, type

```
LIST
```

Or, to get the same listing sent to your printer, type

```
LLIST
```

Remember, as soon as a line that you wish to edit is on the screen, you can move the cursor to it, edit it, and press Enter. If the line is really messed up, you can also reenter it from scratch. To get rid of a line completely, just type and enter its line number, with nothing else on the line.

There are several other versions of both the LIST and LLIST commands that we will cover later in Section 1.

Keystrokes	Description
Arrow keys (← → ↑ ↓)	Used to move the cursor around the screen
Backspace	Used to erase the character to the left of the cursor position
Ctrl + Alt + Del*	Reboots DOS
Ctrl + Break	Interrupts a running program
Ctrl + Home	Clears the monitor screen
Ctrl + J	Used to continue a BASIC line on the next screen line
Ctrl + NumLock	Pauses a running program; hit any key to continue
Ctrl + PrtSc	Provides an echo of screen output to the printer; invoke keystrokes a second time to turn off this feature
Del	Used to erase the character at the cursor position
Enter	Used to enter a line of a program or to execute a command
Esc	Used to erase the line at the cursor position from the screen
Function keys	Used to quickly enter commands
Ins	Used to insert characters at the cursor position
Shift + PrtSc	Outputs whatever is on the screen to the printer

Figure 1-2
Useful keystrokes for working in BASIC.

*Means holding down Ctrl and Alt keys while hitting Del key. The Ctrl, Alt, and Shift keys must always be held down when used in combination with another key. In this table and in this *Guide*, every key preceded by a "+" sign must be held down while striking another key(s).

Some Exercises

Now that you know how to load up BASIC on your computer system and how to issue a few simple BASIC commands, you might try some of the following suggestions:

1. Type and run the BASIC program in Figure 1-1. Did you get the same result as in this guide?
2. Try altering the PRINT statement so that it produces fancier output. For example, to get the computer system to output

   ```
   THE SUM OF 8 AND 16 IS 24
   ```

   your PRINT statement should look like

   ```
   PRINT "THE SUM OF ";NUMBER1;" AND ";NUMBER2;" IS ";SUM
   ```

3. Try making the expression in statement 30 more complicated to see what the effects are. For example, NUMBER1 and NUMBER2 could be multiplied by specifying NUMBER1 * NUMBER2 instead of NUMBER1 + NUMBER2 in statement 30. Note that in BASIC, an asterisk is used to tell the computer to multiply. Multiplication is explained in more detail later.
4. Tinker with the DATA statement by changing the data values (try some negative numbers or numbers with decimal points). Also, experiment to see if it matters where the DATA statement appears. Try placing it as the first, second, or third statement of your program.

A Tougher Example

The program we just looked at was rather simple. The values of the variables didn't change, and the computer wasn't asked to execute a statement out of numerical order. In most programs, however, the values of the variables do change, and the computer is asked to branch to a statement other than the one that immediately follows.

Let's now consider a program that reflects these two added complications. We will write a program to compute and output the squares of 8, 16, and 12.

Designing an Algorithm

Before *coding* (that is, writing out) this problem in BASIC, let's consider what tasks are involved in solving this problem. In addition, let's think about the order in which these tasks must be presented to the computer. The tasks themselves, together with the order in which they are performed, are referred to as an *algorithm*. Designing an algorithm is not that different from building a house. You don't start putting the roof together before you've fully designed the whole structure and decided when the roof will be made relative to other sections.

At first glance, it seems that the following algorithm is attractive for solving our problem:

1. Read a number.
2. Square the number.
3. Print out the result of step 2.
4. Return to step 1.

The fundamental structure involved here is called a *loop*. Thus, the computer system is to read 8, square it (producing 64), output the result (64), loop back to step 1, read 16, square it, and so on. There is one major problem with the four-step solution just described: Once the computer system fully processes the last number (12) and goes back to step 1, there are no more numbers to read. Thus, we need to instruct the loop when to stop. This problem is frequently solved by putting a *trailer* (or *sentinel*) *value* (such as -1) at the end of the data list and directing the computer to leave the loop immediately after this value is read. Thus, we could refine our algorithm as follows:

1. Read a number.
1.5 If the number $= -1$, go to step 5; otherwise process step 2.
2. Square the number.
3. Print out the result of step 2.
4. Return to step 1.
5. End the program.

Although this procedure is complete and produces correct results, many professional programmers include an extra "Read" step to make the procedure *structured*. Many programming languages (such as Pascal and COBOL) make it difficult to code satisfactory programs unless this extra step is taken. As you will learn later on, structured programs result in program logic that is easy to follow.

Inserting the extra Read step (step 3.5) and modifying step 4 so that it points back to step 1.5, we get

1. Read a number.
1.5 If the number $= -1$, go to step 5; otherwise process step 2.
2. Square the number.
3. Print out the result of step 2.
3.5 Read another number.
4. Return to step 1.5.
5. End the program.

Once the algorithm is completely designed, coding it in BASIC becomes relatively straightforward, as you will see by observing the program in Figure 1-3. In this program, the WHILE and WEND statements form a loop that is executed *while* the value of the number is not (i.e. < >) -1. Thus, WHILE and WEND are, respectively, equivalent to steps 1.5 and 4 in the final algorithm just described.

```
10  REM    TITLE:   PROGRAM 1-3
20  REM
30  REM    DESCRIPTION:   THIS PROGRAM READS
40  REM       NUMBERS, SQUARES THEM, AND OUTPUTS
50  REM       THE RESULTS
60  REM
70  REM    AUTHOR: C.S. PARKER
80  REM    DATE: 10/5/91
90  REM
100 REM       NUMBER = THE NUMBER TO BE SQUARED
110 REM       SQUARE = THE SQUARE OF THE NUMBER
120 REM
130 REM    ***********************************
140 READ NUMBER
150 WHILE NUMBER <> -1
160    LET SQUARE=NUMBER^2
170    PRINT "THE SQUARE OF ";NUMBER;" IS";SQUARE
180    READ NUMBER
190 WEND
200 DATA 8,16,12,-1
210 END


RUN
THE SQUARE OF  8  IS 64
THE SQUARE OF  16  IS 256
THE SQUARE OF  12  IS 144
```

Figure 1-3
**A program for computing
and outputting the squares
of several numbers.**

The program in Figure 1-3 has been liberally enhanced with REM statements; remember, these are ignored by the computer. It will take the computer 18 steps to execute this program fully, as shown in Figure 1-4.

Saving and Retrieving

Programs such as the one in Figure 1-3 take some time to create and to successfully get in running order. Hence, when you are through, you may wish to *save* the program and, some time later, *retrieve* it.

Saving is done with the SAVE command. For instance, if we type the command

```
SAVE "SQUARES"
```

at any point when we are entering or editing the program in Figure 1-3, or after we've successfully run it, the computer system will take whatever lines of the program it has in memory and store them on the default disk in a file named SQUARES. The default disk is the one the operating system is currently pointing to, and it is the one identified in the operating system's prompt.

Tomorrow, if you wish to retrieve SQUARES, type

```
LOAD "SQUARES"
```

as soon as you're in BASIC. When the "Ok" message appears on the screen, type LIST to display SQUARES on the screen.

Filenames.   The name that you choose for your program can be any filename that's acceptable to DOS. For example,

Figure 1-4   Steps the computer system must take to fully execute the problem in Figure 1-3.

Step	Statement Executed	Value of NUMBER in Storage	Value of SQUARE in Storage	Action Taken
1	140	8		8 taken from data list and assigned to NUMBER
2	150	8		$8 \neq -1$; therefore, proceed to next statement
3	160	8	64	SQUARE computed
4	170	8	64	Computer system prints THE SQUARE OF 8 IS 64
5	180	16	64	16 taken from data list and assigned to NUMBER
6	190	16	64	Computer directed to line 150
7	150	16	64	$16 \neq -1$; therefore, proceed to next statement
8	160	16	256	SQUARE computed
9	170	16	256	Computer system prints THE SQUARE OF 16 IS 256
10	180	12	256	12 taken from data list and assigned to NUMBER
11	190	12	256	Computer directed to line 150
12	150	12	256	$12 \neq -1$; therefore, proceed to next statement
13	160	12	144	SQUARE computed
14	170	12	144	Computer system prints THE SQUARE OF 12 IS 144
15	180	-1	144	-1 taken from data list and assigned to NUMBER
16	190	-1	144	Computer directed to line 150
17	150	-1	144	$-1 = -1$; therefore, proceed to line 210
18	210	-1	144	The program ends

```
B:SQUARES
B:SQUARES.DAT
A:SQUARES
C:SQUARES
SQUARES
SQUARES.DAT
```

are all acceptable filenames. DOS allows you to name a file with a one- to eight-character filename (the first character of which must be a letter of the alphabet), a one- to three-character filename extension (e.g., DAT), and a one-character disk-drive indicator (e.g., A, B, or C). Both the extension and disk-drive indicator are optional. If no disk-drive indicator is declared, the computer system will automatically go to the default drive to save or look for your file.

The characters allowed in the main part of the filename and the extension are the letters of the alphabet, the digits 0 through 9, and certain special characters. Any lowercase letters of the alphabet typed in a filename will be converted to uppercase characters.

If you do not save a filename with an extension, BASIC will automatically supply the extension .BAS (short for BASIC). You do not need to refer to this extension when you are under the control of BASIC. If you override this extension with one of your own, you must declare that extension whenever you do saving and retrieving operations in BASIC.

Statement and System Commands

There are two major types of commands that you will use to write and run BASIC programs on your computer system: BASIC statement commands and BASIC system commands.

Statement Commands. Statement commands are the commands that are preceded by line numbers. The ones you've encountered so far are REM, LET, READ, DATA, PRINT, END, WHILE, and WEND. These commands instruct the computer what to do while it is executing your program. Subsequent sections of *A Beginner's Guide to BASIC* cover other important statement commands. A summary of statement commands covered in the *Guide* is given in Appendix 1.

System Commands. System commands, in contrast, are designed to tell the computer system to do something before or after it executes a program. The system commands you've encountered so far are RUN, LIST, LLIST, SAVE, and LOAD. Some others that are particularly handy are NEW, RENUM, and SYSTEM. NEW erases memory so that you can work on a fresh program, RENUM renumbers lines of your program (changing all embedded references to these lines as well), and SYSTEM terminates BASIC and returns to the operating system prompt. A more comprehensive list of system commands and several examples of using them are provided in Figure 1-5.

Writing Acceptable BASIC Expressions

Now that we've covered some broad fundamentals concerning how BASIC works, let's consider more closely some rules for writing BASIC instructions. This subsection addresses allowable characters, formation of variables and constants, and the writing of mathematical and logical expressions.

BASIC Character Set

When you are typing in a program, you must use only those characters that are understood by the version of BASIC available to your computer system. Such characters are known as the BASIC *character set*. They fall into three groups:

☐ Alphabetic: ABCDEFGHIJKLMNOPQRSTUVWXYZ

☐ Numeric: 0123456789

☐ Special: ., + & ! < > / @ ( ) — * = (and so on)

Variables

Variables are of two fundamental types: numeric and string. *Numeric variables* can be assigned only numbers, whereas *string variables* can be assigned any combination of alphabetic, numeric, and special characters. Let's look at numeric variables first.

Numeric Variables. The following program contains six numeric variables:

```
10 LET A=6.5
20 LET B=8.04
30 READ C1,C2,C3
40 LET FORMULA=A+B-(C1+C2+C3)
50 PRINT FORMULA
60 DATA 3,2,0.04
70 END
RUN
9.5
```

Figure 1-5
Common usages of BASIC
system commands.

AUTO

Automatically supplies line numbers so that you don't have to type them in. Examples:

AUTO	Numbers lines in increments of 10, starting with line 10 (i.e., 10, 20, 30, . . .)
AUTO 100	Numbers lines in increments of 10, starting with line 100 (i.e., 100, 110, 120, . . .)

To terminate automatic line numbering, press down the Control key while hitting the Break key.

DELETE

Used to delete lines of a program. Examples:

DELETE 20	Deletes only line 20
DELETE 20-100	Deletes lines 20 through 100
DELETE 50-	Deletes from line 50 on
DELETE -50	Deletes all lines up to and including line 50

FILES

Lists the names of all files mounted on a particular disk drive. Examples:

FILES "*.BAS"	Lists the names of all BASIC files on the default drive
FILES "B:"	Lists the names of all files on the B drive

KILL

Used to erase a file from disk. Example: KILL "FRED" kills a file named FRED.BAS on disk.

LIST

Used to output the lines of a program on the display screen. Examples:

LIST	Lists the entire program
LIST 20	Lists only line 20
LIST 20-100	Lists lines 20 through 100
LIST 50-	Lists from line 50 on
LIST -50	Lists all lines up to and including line 50

LLIST

Used to output the lines of a program on the printer. For examples, see the "LIST" command above. (Note: You must change the keyword LIST to LLIST to get these to work.)

Each variable (A, B, C1, C2, C3, and FORMULA) is allocated a storage location by the computer at execution time. Each location may store a number while your program is executing.

Versions of BASIC vary somewhat in the way numeric variable names may be created by the programmer. In most versions of BASIC, variable names are made up of letters of the alphabet, the digits 0 through 9, and the decimal point. The following rules are in effect for naming numeric variables:

1. A variable name must begin with a letter of the alphabet.
2. A variable name cannot be more than 40 characters long.
3. The decimal point is used as a separator character in a variable name. Other characters used by other languages for this purpose, such as hyphens and underscores, are not allowed.
4. A variable name cannot be a reserved word. Reserved words are names that BASIC uses for its own needs. A complete list of reserved words is given in Appendix 2.

Some examples of acceptable variable names are:

LOAD

Figure 1-5
continued

Used to retrieve a program from disk and place it into memory. Examples:

```
LOAD "JOHN"         Retrieves JOHN.BAS from the default drive
LOAD "JOHN.22"      Retrieves JOHN.22 from the default drive
LOAD "B:JOHN.22"    Retrieves JOHN.22 from drive B
```

NEW

Clears current program from computer memory, enabling a fresh program to be typed in.
Example: NEW

RENUM

Used to renumber program lines. Examples:

```
RENUM       Renumbers in increments of 10, starting at 100 (i.e., 100,
            110, 120, . . .)
RENUM 10    Renumbers in increments of 10, starting at 10 (i.e., 10, 20,
            30, . . .)
```

RUN

Executes a program. Example: RUN PAYROLL runs a program called PAYROLL.BAS.

SAVE

Writes the program that is currently stored in memory onto disk. Examples:

```
SAVE "JOHN"         Saves program as JOHN.BAS on the default drive
SAVE "JOHN.22"      Saves program as JOHN.22 on the default drive
SAVE "B:JOHN.22"    Saves program as JOHN.22 on the B drive
```

SYSTEM

Automatically returns to the operating system. Example: SYSTEM

TRON and TROFF

Used for debugging purposes to trace the order in which lines have been processed in a
program. Typing TRON before you run a program turns the trace feature on; typing TROFF
anytime thereafter turns the feature off. Example: Typing TRON before you ran the program
in Figure 1-1 would produce [10] [20] [30] [40] [60] as output.

```
TOM
AMOUNTDUE
AMOUNT.DUE
AMOUNT.DUE.NOW
DAYS.1
I
A1
```

Some examples of invalid names are:

```
$I             Does not begin with a letter
NAME           NAME is a reserved word
AMOUNT-DUE     The hyphen is not allowed
```

It is highly advisable to choose descriptive variable names so that you won't
forget what they represent. The programs in the figures in the *Guide* generally
use descriptive names. In the short example programs, however, we will often
resort to shorter names so you can quickly see how a statement or function works.

String Variables.   A *string* is a collection of related characters; for example,

```
JOHN Q. DOE
1600 Pennsylvania Avenue
THX-1138
```

Strings may be assigned to variable names and manipulated by computer systems. Strings can contain uppercase and/or lowercase characters, and these characters are output exactly as they are entered. The following program contains only string variables:

```
10 LET A$="at this example"
20 LET B$="LOOK CAREFULLY "
30 PRINT B$;A$
40 END
RUN
LOOK CAREFULLY at this example
```

There are two string variables in this short program: A$ and B$. The computer allocates storage space to string variables in essentially the same way it allocates storage to numeric variables. In other words, the storage location set up for A$ contains the string

```
at this example
```

and the location set up for B$ contains the string

```
LOOK CAREFULLYb      (b represents a blank space)
```

Since A$ and B$ are variables, they can contain different strings throughout the course of the program but only one string at any given time. An important difference between numeric and string variables is that we can perform conventional arithmetic with numeric variables but generally not with string ones.

Names for string variables are formed under the same set of rules as numeric variables, with one exception. As you've probably already noticed, string variables always end with a $ sign.

Many computer systems require that the string assigned to a string variable be enclosed in quotes; for example,

```
10 READ A$
20 PRINT A$
30 DATA "EVERY GOOD STUDENT DOES FINE"
40 END
RUN
EVERY GOOD STUDENT DOES FINE
```

Constants

Like their variable counterparts, *constants* may be either numeric or string. Unlike variables, however, the value of a constant doesn't change (although constants can be assigned to variables, which can change).

Numeric Constants.   A *numeric constant* is simply a number—for example, 81, −54, .001. When creating arithmetic expressions in BASIC, it is often useful to assign numbers to or to use numbers in combination with numeric variables. Some examples are

□   `10 LET A=5.0`   5.0 is a numeric constant

□   `10 LET B=A+2`   2 is a numeric constant

□   `10 LET C=.01*A+B`   .01 is a numeric constant

Although the numeric constant chosen can be an integer number or a number with a decimal point, the use of commas or dollar signs is not allowed as part of the constant itself. The following are invalid representations of numeric constants in a BASIC program:

□   `10 LET A=2,000`   Comma invalid; LET A = 2000 valid

□   `100 DATA $6,$3.52` $ invalid; DATA 6,3.52 valid

In many cases we would like to precede a number by a $ sign. This can be done very simply, as the following short example suggests:

```
10 LET A=5.21
20 PRINT "$";A
30 END
RUN
$ 5.21
```

String Constants.   A *string constant*, or *literal*, is simply any collection of allowable BASIC characters enclosed in quotes; for example,

```
"HELLO 12?"
"GOODBYE MY LOVELY"
"145-86-7777"
"Mr. William T. Jones"
```

String constants can be assigned to string variables, such as

```
10 LET A$="EVERY GOOD STUDENT DOES FINE"
```

or be declared independently of any variables, as in the following PRINT statement:

```
10 PRINT "The value of inventory is $";X
```

On many computer systems, string constants appearing in DATA statements need not be enclosed in quotes.

Expressions

Expressions in BASIC are one of two principal types—arithmetic and relational.

Arithmetic Expressions.   Arithmetic expressions are combinations of arithmetic symbols, numeric variables, and numeric constants that evaluate to a numeric value. For instance, the expression

```
A+2
```

which consists of a numeric variable, the plus symbol, and the numeric constant 2, respectively, is an arithmetic expression. If A = 1, the expression has a value of 3. The following operations are permitted in arithmetic expressions:

Operation	BASIC Symbol Used
Addition	+
Subtraction	−
Multiplication	*
Division	/
Exponentiation	^

For example, suppose A = 1, B = 3, and C = 2. The following statements would produce the results indicated:

☐   `10 LET D=A+B-C`   D is assigned a value of 2. The previous value of D is lost.

☐   `10 LET C=B/2`   The right-hand side equals 1.5, which is assigned to C. The previous value of C is lost.

☐   `10 PRINT A*B`   A and B are multiplied, and the product, 3, is printed.

Now consider a more complicated expression, such as:

$$10 \ LET \ D=C-A+B/(C+4)^2$$

The question arises here as to which operation the computer will perform first. BASIC and many other languages recognize the following order of arithmetic operations:

1.   All operations within parentheses are performed first, starting with the innermost set of parentheses.
2.   Exponentiation is performed next.
3.   Multiplication and division are performed next, and the computer executes these from left to right in the expression.
4.   Addition and subtraction are performed last, also left to right.

Thus, the expression just given would be evaluated as follows under this set of rules:

Step	Operation Performed
1	(C+4) evaluated; result is 6
2	6^2 evaluated; result is 36
3	B/36 evaluated; result is .083333
4	C−A evaluated; result is 1
5	1 is added to .083333; result is 1.083333
6	D is assigned the value 1.083333; the previous value of D is lost

To be fully sure that you understand the order of arithmetic operations, you should study the following examples. Assume in the examples that W = 1, X = 2, Y = 3, and Z = 4.

Example 1   `10 LET A=Y/W*Z`
A would be assigned a value of 12, since division and multiplication, being on the same level of hierarchy, are performed left to right.

Example 2   `10 LET B=(X+Y)*(W+1)^2`
B would be assigned a value of 20. Parenthetical expressions are evaluated first, then exponentiation, and finally multiplication.

Example 3   `LET C=((Z-W)*X)^2/2`
C would be assigned a value of 18. The computation in the innermost parentheses is performed first, yielding $Z-W=3$. Then contents of the outermost parentheses are evaluated, yielding $3*2=6$. After all of the parenthetical expressions are evaluated, the 6 is squared. Finally, the result of all the previous operations, 36, is halved to produce 18.

Relational Expressions.   Relational expressions are combinations of variables, symbols, and constants that evaluate to a value of "true" or "false." For example,

`NUMBER=-1`

is a relational expression that is true when NUMBER is -1 and false otherwise.
    There are six relational operators that are used in relational expressions:

Relational Meaning	Operator
Equal to	=
Not equal to	<> or ><
Greater than	>
Less than	<
Greater than or equal to	>= or =>
Less than or equal to	<= or =<

Some examples of the use of relational operators follow. Assume in the examples that SEX\$ = "FEMALE" and X = 25.

☐   `WHILE SEX$ = "MALE"`   Evaluates to false

☐   `WHILE SEX$ = "Female"`   Evaluates to false

☐   `WHILE SEX$ = "FEMALE"`   Evaluates to true

☐   `WHILE SEX$ <> "MALE"`   Evaluates to true

☐   `WHILE X >= 25`   Evaluates to true

☐   `WHILE X > 25`   Evaluates to false

The WHILE and IF statements are the two major important statements in BASIC that use relational expressions. Later in this section you will learn how to use the IF statement.

Logical Connectives.   Relational expressions can be made more powerful through the use of the three reserved connective words: NOT, AND, and OR.
    Preceding a relational expression with the NOT connective negates the condition. So, for instance, the relational expression

`NOT SEX$ = "MALE"`

is true if SEX$ carries any value other than MALE, and the relational expression

```
NOT A = 6
```

is true if A is any value other than 6.

The AND connective links two or more conditions in a compound expression. AND requires that all conditions be true for the entire expression to be true. It works as follows:

```
SEX$ = "MALE" AND A = 6
```

means that *both* SEX$ has to be MALE and A has to be 6 for the entire compound expression to be true. And,

```
A = 1 AND B = 6 AND C = 35
```

means that all three conditions have to be true for the compound expression to be true. If A = 1 and B = 6 but C = 34, the compound expression would be false.

The OR connective means that one or more of the conditions in a compound expression must be true in order for the expression to be true. For instance, the compound expression

```
A = 1 OR B = 6
```

is true if either one of the two conditions, or both of them, are true. Like AND, more than one OR can exist to link conditions that are part of a compound expression.

NOT, AND, and OR can be combined to form a compound expression. If you are doing this, it's advisable that you put parentheses around like subexpressions to minimize complexity. As with arithmetic expressions, whatever is in parentheses is evaluated first. For instance, the expression

```
NOT (TYPE = 1 OR TYPE = 2)
```

will be true if TYPE is not equal to 1 or 2. Similarly,

```
A = 6 AND (B = 4 OR C = 88)
```

will be true only if A is 6 and one of the following: (1) B is 4 but C is not 88, (2) C is 88 but B is not 4, and (3) both B is 4 and C is 88. In the absence of parentheses, the connectives are evaluated in the following order: NOT, AND, OR.

Hierarchy of Operations.   As you've learned here, expressions can be formed through a variety of symbols. When these are mixed, the following order is observed:

Order	Operation	Symbols
1	Parentheses	( )
2	Arithmetic operators	^ * / + −
3	Relational operators	= < > <> <= >=
4	Connectives	NOT AND OR

More on Elementary BASIC Statements

So far, we've informally shown the use of the REM, READ and DATA, WHILE and WEND, LET, PRINT, and END statements. Let's consider further the permissible usage of these statements.

READ and DATA Statements

As mentioned earlier, the READ and DATA statements are always used together. When a READ is executed, the computer will assign values appearing in the DATA statements to the respective variables named in the READ statement. The format of each of these statements is shown below:

```
Line #   READ list of variables (separated by commas)
Line #   DATA list of data items (separated by commas)
```

The DATA statements are never actually executed by the computer. Between the time the RUN command is issued and the program is executed, the computer system extracts all of the values from the DATA statements and prepares a "data list." It is this list that is referenced each time a READ is encountered. The DATA statement itself is ignored during program execution.

It is useful to think of a "pointer" attached to the data list. The pointer initially points to the first value in the data list. When this value is assigned, it then points to the second item, and so on. For example, consider the READ and DATA statements for the program in Figure 1-3. The pointer initially points to the 8. When statement 140 is executed, the 8 is assigned to NUMBER and the pointer moves to the 16; when the next READ (statement 180) is executed, 16 is assigned to NUMBER (the previous value, 8, being erased) and the pointer moves to the 12; and so on. When the -1 is finally assigned to NUMBER, the data list is exhausted.

There can be several DATA statements in a BASIC program, a fact that is observable in the solved review problems at the end of the section. In most implementations of BASIC, DATA statements can be placed anywhere before the END statement. It is critical to keep in mind that data are executed in the order in which they appear in the DATA statements, and if there are several DATA statements, the earliest of these will be used first.

LET Statement

The LET statement typically uses the following format:

```
Line # LET variable-name = expression
```

An important requirement of this format is that only a single variable name is allowed to appear on the left-hand side of the = sign. Thus,

```
10 LET A=6*B-C^(N-1)
10 LET D=0
```

are allowable, whereas

```
LET A+B=C
```

is not. A single variable must appear on the left-hand side because once the right-hand-side expression is computed down to a single value, a storage location (as represented by a single variable) must be declared to store this value. Remember, A, B, C, and so on are acceptable names for storage locations, whereas A + B is not.

The = sign of the LET statement is referred to as an *assignment* (or *replacement*) *symbol*. In a LET statement, = does not mean "is equal to," the relational operator. To understand the basis of this nomenclature, consider the perfectly acceptable BASIC statement

$$10 \text{ LET } I = I + 1$$

This statement makes absolutely no sense if we interpret the = sign as meaning "is equal to." However, if we interpret this statement as instructing the computer to determine the value of I + 1 and to assign the number obtained back to I, it does make sense. Thus, if the value 6 were initially stored in I, this statement would add 6 to 1 and assign the result, 7, back to I (erasing the 6 that was there previously).

In most versions of BASIC, the appearance of the word LET is optional in a LET statement. Thus,

$$10 \text{ } I = I + 1$$

is perfectly acceptable.

PRINT Statement

The PRINT statement, being the main vehicle for obtaining BASIC output, is so pivotal that a separate section in the *Guide* is devoted exclusively to its use (see Section 4). So far we have seen that one acceptable form of the PRINT statement is

$$\text{Line \# PRINT} \begin{Bmatrix} \text{literal,} \\ \text{variable, or} \\ \text{expression} \end{Bmatrix}; \begin{Bmatrix} \text{literal,} \\ \text{variable, or} \\ \text{expression} \end{Bmatrix}; \dots$$

Thus, the following statements are allowable:

□ 50 PRINT "A=";A
   If 6 is stored in A, the output is
   A = 6

□ 50 PRINT A;B;C*Z;M$
   If 6 is stored in A, 72 in B, 16 in C, 2 in Z, and " ARE THE ANSWERS" in M$, the output is
   6 72 32 ARE THE ANSWERS

□ 50 PRINT A$;B$
   If "HIGH " is stored in A$ and "SCHOOL" in B$, the output is
   HIGH SCHOOL

Other versions of the PRINT statement are covered in Section 4.

WHILE and WEND Statements

WHILE and WEND are companion statements that form a loop. WHILE represents the beginning of the loop; WEND represents the end. For sake of program readability, statements within a loop are normally indented, as shown in Figure 1-3 (lines 160 through 180).

The formats of the WHILE and WEND statements are as follows.

```
Line # WHILE relational-expression
        .
        .
        .
Line # WEND
```

On each loop iteration, before execution of statements within the loop takes place, the computer system checks to see if the relational expression contained in the WHILE statement is true or false. If the expression is true, all of the statements within the loop are executed in the order suggested by the line numbers. Then the expression is checked again, before the next loop iteration. As soon as the relational expression returns a value of "false," control is passed to the statement that follows the loop (i.e., the statement that follows the WEND statement).

It is also possible to have loops within loops; that is, loops formed by WHILE and WEND statements can be nested. For example,

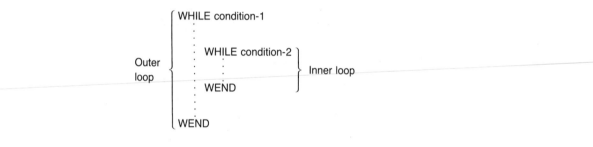

The rules for nesting WHILE/WEND loops are similar to those of FOR/NEXT loops, which we'll cover in Section 3.

IF Statement

The IF statement follows the format shown below:

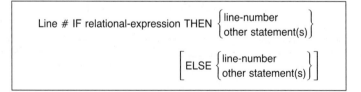

The computer executes an IF statement as follows:

1. The relational expression is evaluated as true or false.
2. In the case where there is no ELSE clause, if the expression is true, the computer does whatever action is specified after the THEN clause; otherwise, the computer advances to the next statement.

3. In the case where there is an ELSE clause, if the expression is true, the computer does whatever action is specified after the THEN clause; otherwise, it does whatever action is specified after the ELSE clause.

Sometimes, the two forms of the IF statement are differentiated by referring to the "IF without ELSE" version as the IF-THEN statement and the "IF with ELSE" version as the "IF-THEN-ELSE" statement. We will now consider each of these forms in turn.

IF-THEN.   The following shows some acceptable forms of IF-THEN:

☐   ```
10 IF A > B THEN 170
20 ...
```
The computer goes to statement 170 if A > B; otherwise, it goes to statement 20.

☐    ```
10 IF A > B THEN C = C + 1
20 ...
```
If A > B, the computer calculates C + 1 and puts the value in C; then, it goes to statement 20. If A is not greater than B, the computer goes directly to statement 20, bypassing the calculation.

☐   ```
10 IF CUSTOMER$ <> "LAST RECORD" THEN 50
20 ...
```
The computer goes to statement 50 if CUSTOMER$ does not have a value of LAST RECORD; otherwise, it goes to statement 20.

**IF-THEN-ELSE.**    Below is an example of the IF-THEN-ELSE statement used to award a $50 bonus to salespeople selling $5,000 or more worth of merchandise:

```
20 IF S >= 5000 THEN B = 50
              ELSE B = 0
30 ...
```

In this statement, the relational expression S >= 5000 is first evaluated. If the expression is true, then B is set to 50; otherwise, B is set to 0. Regardless of the value B is given, after statement 20 is executed, the computer goes to statement 30.

While statement 20 could have been written in a single line, it is good programming practice to tier the THEN and ELSE clauses in the manner shown. To get to the second line of statement 20, use either the Line Feed key on your keyboard or press down the Control (Ctrl) key while hitting the J key. In either case, the screen cursor advances to the second line of statement 20, where you can type the ELSE clause. After finishing the second line, press the Enter key. Do not press Enter after the first line, because the computer will assume you are finished with it and will place it in memory.

In some programs that you write, you may want to execute two or more statements if the value of a relational expression is true or, possibly, two or more statements if the value is false. For example, suppose the salesperson selling $5,000 or more worth of merchandise is given both a bonus of $50 and a watch (W$ = "YES"). We might then code the statement given earlier to inform us of this information as follows:
```

Figure 1-6 Use of the IF-THEN-ELSE form of IF statement.

```
10  REM     TITLE:   PROGRAM 1-6
20  REM
30  REM     DESCRIPTION:   READS A LIST OF NUMBERS
40  REM        AND TELLS WHETHER EACH NUMBER IS
50  REM        POSITIVE OR NEGATIVE
60  REM
70  REM     AUTHOR: C.S. PARKER
80  REM     DATE: 10/5/91
90  REM
100 REM     NUMBER = A POSITIVE OR NEGATIVE NUMBER
110 REM     SIGN$  = SIGN OF THE NUMBER
120 REM
130 REM     ***********************************
140 READ NUMBER
150 WHILE NUMBER <> 0
160     IF NUMBER < 0 THEN SIGN$ = "NEGATIVE"           ◄─── IF statement
                      ELSE SIGN$ = "POSITIVE"
170     PRINT NUMBER; "IS ";SIGN$
180     READ NUMBER
190 WEND
200 DATA 8,-16,-65,12,0
210 END

RUN
  8 IS POSITIVE
-16 IS NEGATIVE
-65 IS NEGATIVE
 12 IS POSITIVE
```

```
100 IF S>=5000 THEN B=50:W$="YES"
              ELSE B=0:W$="NO"
```

On many computer systems, the colon character (:) is used, as shown above, to separate statements appearing on the same line.

Figure 1-6 provides a full program that shows how IF-THEN-ELSE is used. This program reads a series of numbers, determines whether each number is positive or negative, and outputs the result. In this program, a trailer value of 0 is used to indicate the end of the file.

REM Statement

The REM (remark) statement is a very important tool in BASIC, even though it is completely ignored by the computer when the program is executed. Its purpose is to allow you to put useful comments, or blank lines, in the program listing. The format of the REM statement is

> Line # REM any remark

REMs can appear anywhere in a program. In many versions of BASIC, they must appear before the END statement.

END Statement

Generally the END statement is physically the last statement in the program; that is, it is the statement with the highest line number. When the computer encounters this statement, it terminates execution of your program. The format of the END statement is

Line # END

Some versions of BASIC do not require an END statement; however, its use is highly recommended, because it leaves no doubt in anyone's mind about where the program ends. The END statement is frequently used in combination with the STOP statement. The STOP statement is discussed in Section 3.

Developing BASIC Programs

Now that we've covered how to write simple BASIC programs, it's time to consider how to develop them on your computer system.

Let's say you want to "try out" your computer system by typing in the squares program of Figure 1-3. You would type in all 21 lines, pressing the Enter key after finishing each line, as usual. Many versions of BASIC will check each statement for correct form (or *syntax*) when you press Enter. Thus, suppose you fumble at the keyboard while typing in the fourteenth line of your program, producing

```
140 READD NUMBER
```

Your keyboard has a set of arrow keys, a Delete key, and a Backspace key that will let you fix the error if you have not hit the Enter key. If you have already hit the Enter key to send the faulty line to the computer system, the following error message might be sent to the output device:

```
Syntax error in 140
```

At this point, list line 140 (if it isn't already on the screen), use the arrow and editing keys to go to and correct the error, and enter the change with the Enter key. The computer system will then replace the old line 140 with the corrected version.

When you have finished typing your program, you probably will be anxious for the computer to execute it immediately. Most systems require the user to type in the command

```
RUN
```

After you issue this command, one of the following will happen:

1. The program will run successfully, producing the correct answers.
2. The program will run but produce incorrect answers. This might happen if, for example, you typed in line 160 of the squares program as

```
160 LET SQUARE=NUMBER^3
```

The program would then produce cubes of numbers instead of squares! Thus, it is important that you look at your output carefully before you decide that your program works.

3.   The program stops unexpectedly in the middle of a run. This would happen in the squares program if line 200 were typed in as follows:

```
200 DATA 8,16,"HELLO",12,-1
```

The program would compute the squares of 8 and 16 successfully, but it would stop (or abort) when it tried to assign the string "HELLO" to the numeric variable NUMBER. When BASIC runs into this situation while running the program, it is likely to display a message such as

```
Syntax error in 200
```

and halt. At this point you must correct the error, or *bug*, in the program and try again. Learning how to correct, or *debug*, faulty programs is one of the most important skills you must develop to program well. As unusual as it may seem, even a good programmer can easily spend 50 percent of the time it takes to develop a program in getting rid of bugs in it. This subject will be addressed in more detail later on.

Solved Review Problems

Example 1

A company has anywhere from five to twenty students employed on a part-time basis during the summer. This past week, five students were on the payroll. The students each worked different hours at different rates of pay, as shown in the following table:

Student Name	Hours Worked	Rate of Pay
John Smith	20	$5.40
Nancy Jones	15	$5.60
Bo Weeks	25	$5.00
Millicent Smythe	40	$4.80
Thu Duoc	20	$5.10

The company would like you to write a BASIC program to compute and print the total pay earned by each student.

Solution

The program must successively read a number of *records*. Consequently, a looping structure similar to the one in the program of Figure 1-3 will be required. Each record will contain a name, the hours worked, and a rate of pay—that is, a row of data from the preceding table. The number of records varies from week to week, so it will be convenient to employ a trailer record to enable the program to terminate. These considerations lead to the program in Figure 1-7, which you should study carefully.

Before we leave this example, let's consider some of the problems we might have run into if there were errors in the program. Also, we'll explore how we might correct such errors.

Figure 1-7
A program for computing the
pay owed to employees.

```
10    REM     TITLE:    PROGRAM 1-7
20    REM
30    REM     DESCRIPTION: THIS PROGRAM
40    REM        COMPUTES EMPLOYEE PAY
50    REM
60    REM     AUTHOR: C.S. PARKER
70    REM     DATE: 10/5/91
80    REM
90    REM     EMPLOYEE$ = EMPLOYEE NAME
100   REM     HOURS     = HOURS WORKED
110   REM     PAY       = HOURLY PAY RATE
120   REM     PAYDUE    = PAY DUE
130   REM
140   REM********************************
150   READ EMPLOYEE$,HOURS,PAY
160   WHILE EMPLOYEE$ <> "LAST RECORD"
170      PAYDUE = HOURS * PAY
180      PRINT EMPLOYEE$;" HAS EARNED   $";PAYDUE
190      READ EMPLOYEE$,HOURS,PAY
200   WEND
210   REM ********DATA STATEMENTS*********
220   DATA "JOHN SMITH",20,5.40
230   DATA "NANCY JONES",15,5.60
240   DATA "BO WEEKS",25,5.00
250   DATA "MILLICENT SMYTHE",40,4.80
260   DATA "THU DUOC",20,5.10
270   DATA "LAST RECORD",0,0
280   REM ********************************
290   END

RUN
JOHN SMITH HAS EARNED   $ 108
NANCY JONES HAS EARNED   $ 84
BO WEEKS HAS EARNED   $ 125
MILLICENT SMYTHE HAS EARNED   $ 192
THU DUOC HAS EARNED   $ 102
```

First, suppose we had mistyped line 170 as follows:

```
170 PAYDUE = HRS * PAY
```

When the computer encounters this statement, it has a value for HOURS and PAY. However, it doesn't have a clue as to what HRS is, since we never assigned a value to it. In most versions of BASIC, when the computer is asked to use the value of a variable that it has not yet encountered during execution, it assumes the value is zero. Naturally, this can lead to some very surprising results in your programs. In the current problem, your program would show that everyone has earned $0.

You should quickly be able to find an error like the one just described by making a few simple deductions. For example, since all the values of PAYDUE are printing as 0 and PAYDUE is supposed to be computed by HOURS*PAY, either HOURS or PAY (or both of these variables) is equal to zero.

As a second example, suppose we had mistakenly typed in line 250 as follows:

```
250 DATA 40,"MILLICENT SMYTHE",4.80
```

The computer would execute our program successfully until it had printed out

```
BO WEEKS HAS EARNED $125
```

Then we might receive a message such as the following:

```
Syntax error on line 250
```

These two lines of output give us a clue to the error. The computer successfully completed the processing of Bo Weeks's record but subsequently "bombed" on line 250. Thus, something must be amiss with the data in the next record. Now we would notice that the number 40 and "MILLICENT SMYTHE" are switched around, and BASIC cannot assign a string constant to a numeric variable.

Debugging programs is a skill that involves a lot of practice. You must learn to make deductions from the information given by the computer system (i.e., partial output, incorrect output, and error messages) to determine the source of errors.

Another technique that's recommended for particularly hard-to-find errors is the so-called dummy (diagnostic) PRINT statement. Suppose again that for line 170 you had typed

```
170 PAYDUE = HRS * PAY
```

You have deduced that either HRS, PAY, or both of these variables are zero, but you still can't put your finger on the error. However, you could now type the statement

```
175 PRINT "HRS = "; HRS;" PAY = "; PAY
```

The computer system would then respond with the following outputs after you typed RUN:

```
HRS = 0   PAY = 5.40
JOHN SMITH HAS EARNED   $ 0
HRS = 0   PAY = 5.60
NANCY JONES HAS EARNED   $ 0
```

and so on. Now the source of the error is obvious: HRS is zero for every record in the program.

Once the dummy PRINT statement has served its purpose of uncovering the error and the error has been corrected, statement 175 should be deleted so that it won't interfere with the normal output of the program. The form for doing this is

```
DELETE 175
```

on your system, or you can type simply

```
175
```

and press Enter.

Figure 1-8
A selection program.

```
10  REM     TITLE:   PROGRAM 1-8
20  REM
30  REM     DESCRIPTION: THIS PROGRAM SELECTS FROM
40  REM        A FILE ALL FEMALE EMPLOYEES OVER 40
50  REM          WHO WORK IN THE ACCOUNTING DEPARTMENT
60  REM
70  REM     AUTHOR - C.S. PARKER
80  REM     DATE: 10/5/91
90  REM
100 REM     EMPLOYEE$ = EMPLOYEE NAME
110 REM     SEX$      = SEX
120 REM     AGE       = AGE
130 REM     DEPT$     = DEPARTMENT
140 REM
150 REM *********************************
160 READ EMPLOYEE$,SEX$,AGE,DEPT$
170 WHILE EMPLOYEE$ <> "LAST RECORD"
180     IF SEX$ = "MALE" THEN 220
190     IF AGE <= 40 THEN 220
200     IF DEPT$ <> "ACCOUNTING" THEN 220
210     PRINT EMPLOYEE$
220     READ EMPLOYEE$,SEX$,AGE,DEPT$
230 WEND
240 REM **********DATA STATEMENTS**********
250 DATA "JANE CRIBBS","FEMALE",25,"ACCOUNTING"
260 DATA "PHIL JONES","MALE",45,"ACCOUNTING"
270 DATA "ANNE WELLES","FEMALE",42,"ACCOUNTING"
280 DATA "MARY SMITH","FEMALE",41,"FINANCE"
290 DATA "LAST RECORD","MALE",99,"NONE"
300 REM *********************************
310 END

RUN
ANNE WELLES
```

Example 2
ABC Company has a file that keeps the following information on employees:

☐   Name   ☐   Age

☐   Sex (M or F)   ☐   Department

The file has approximately 1,000 employees, although the exact number is usually unknown. Write a BASIC program that will print out the names of all females over age 40 who work in the accounting department.

Solution
This program involves a series of three IF statements that pose the three conditions we wish to check in each record—in other words, female?, over 40?, and accounting? If a record passes all three checks, we print the associated name; otherwise we immediately read the next record.

Since the data file is not given, we'll make up five test records (including a trailer record) to illustrate how the program works. The program is shown in Figure 1-8.

Exercises

Instructions: Provide an answer to each of the following questions.

1. Categorize the following variables as numeric, string, or invalid:
   a. A　　　　b. 6F　　　　c. D1　　　　d. B$　　　　e. $R　　　　f. I

2. Write a valid LET statement for each of the following formulas:

   a. $C = A^2 + B^2$　　　　c. $R = \dfrac{S + T}{U - V} - Y$

   b. $A = \left(\dfrac{B + C}{D}\right)E$　　　　d. $A = \dfrac{3(B - 1)}{T + 2}$

3. Given $A = 2$, $B = 5$, and $C = 6$, determine the value of X in the following BASIC expressions:
   a. `X=(A+B)*C`　　　　c. `X=(A+C/A+1)^2/2`
   b. `X=C/A*B`　　　　　d. `X=((3*A)*B)/C-4`

4. Identify the syntax errors, if any, in the following BASIC statements:
   a. `10 LET X+Y=Z`
   b. `98 IF X-Y<=C-D THEN 200`
   c. `20 LET F$=F+5.23`

5. In the expression

$$X=(Y+Z)^2-2*B$$

   which operation does the computer do
   a. first?　　　　c. third?
   b. second?　　　　d. last?

6. Determine whether the following relational expressions are true or false. Assume that $A = 1$, $B = 6$, $C = 2$, CUSTOMER$ = "Smith", and TYPE = 3.
   a. `A = 1 OR B = 2`
   b. `A = 2 AND B = 6`
   c. `NOT (TYPE = 1 OR TYPE = 2)`
   d. `A = 1 AND (B = 2 OR C = 2)`
   e. `CUSTOMER$ = "SMITH"`
   f. `A = 1 OR (B = 7 AND C = 1)`

Programming Problems

Instructions: Write a BASIC program to do each of the following tasks.

1. Find the sum of each of the following pairs of numbers.

6 and	8
13 and	25
14 and	33
19 and	41

   Use trailer values at the end of your data list so that your program can sense when there are no more data.

2. Following are three sets of data. Each set of data has four variables: A, B, C, and D:

	Variables			
Set	A	B	C	D
1	8	15	10	4
2	6	5	3	2
3	4	0	5	2

Plug the values in each set of data into the following formula, and print out the results:

$$X = A - B * C + A / D$$

3. Salespeople at XYZ Company are paid a base salary of $10,000. This salary may be augmented by commissions, which are equal to 10 percent of gross sales, and by a bonus of $500. The bonus is awarded only to salespeople with more than $80,000 in gross sales. Compute and output the amounts earned by each of these salespeople:

Salesperson	Gross Sales
Carlos Ortiz	$90,000
Jill Johnson	$70,000
Don Williams	$20,000
Dee Jones	$95,000
Al Ennis	$40,000

Your output should include the name of each salesperson and his or her earnings. Use trailer values at the end of your data list so that your program can sense when there are no more data.

4. Solve Problem 3 assuming that the commission is computed as follows:

If Gross Sales Are in the Range of	The Commission Rate Is
$ 1–$30,000	6%
$30,001–$60,000	8%
$60,001–$80,000	10%
$80,001 and above	12%

Assume also that the bonus is still in effect.

5. Grades in a course are awarded as follows: 90 and above = A, 80–89 = B, 70–79 = C, 60–69 = D, below 60 = F. Write a BASIC program that reads the following data and assigns letter grades:

Social Security Number	Score
182-66-1919	63
321-76-4344	81
821-66-0045	90
376-38-3202	54
802-11-1481	79
346-49-8911	75

Your output should include the social security number of each student and that student's letter grade. Use trailer values at the end of your data list so that your program can sense when there are no more items to be read.

6.   A company running a copying service charges the following rates:

> The first 500 copies are billed at 5 cents per copy
> The next 500 copies are billed at 4 cents per copy
> Any additional copies are billed at 3 cents per copy

Compute and output the amount each of the following customers is to be billed:

Customer	Copies
XYZ Amalgamated	1,200
ABC Industries	200
TR Systems Limited	800

Your output should include the name of each customer as well as the billing amount. Use trailer values at the end of your data list so that your program can sense when there are no more data.

7.   Students at a university are billed as follows:

$$\text{Tuition} = \$100 \text{ per credit hour}$$
$$\text{Activity fee} = \begin{array}{l} \$30 \text{ for 6 hours or less} \\ \$60 \text{ for 7--12 hours} \\ \$75 \text{ for more than 12 hours} \end{array}$$

The total amount a student will be billed each semester is computed by the following formula:

$$\text{Tuition fee} + \text{Activity fee} - \text{Scholarship}$$

Compute the amounts due from the following students:

Student Name	Credit Hours This Semester	Scholarship Amount
Ed Begay	15	$700
Bill Mendoza	8	0
John Williams	3	0
Nancy Jones	12	500
Dennis Hall	6	0

Your output should include the name of each student as well as the billing amount. Use trailer values at the end of your data list so that your program can sense when there are no more data.

8.   Workers at a factory receive "time and a half" for every hour worked over 40 hours in any week. That is, workers are paid 150 percent of their regular hourly rate for each hour worked beyond the 40-hour mark. Read the following employee records for the first week of January and compute the total pay owed to each employee.

Employee	Hours Worked	Rate Class
S. Akins	40	A
F. Baker	45	C
M. Chang	48	B
A. Faziz	35	A
J. Tate	40	C
L. Yev	42	B

Note that the following rate classes are in effect:

□   Class A workers make $14.00 per hour

□   Class B workers make $11.00 per hour

□   Class C workers make $10.00 per hour

Section 2
Program Design Techniques

Introduction

As mentioned earlier, the design of computer programs requires considerable care. Programs used to help run businesses are usually in operation for several years, and they need to be constantly modified to meet changing business conditions. Thus, a program that is designed in a hasty fashion will often cause numerous maintenance problems over the years for programmers who have to keep it up to date. Simply stated, poorly designed programs are almost always expensive headaches. A few extra dollars spent on initial design may save hundreds of dollars later.

Many techniques have been employed over the years to design computer programs. Two of the most widely used techniques are flowcharts and pseudocode.

Flowcharts and Pseudocode

Program flowcharts, dating back to the 1940s, are among the oldest tools used to design programs. A program flowchart is a diagram that shows the flow of logic behind a computer program. For example, the flowchart in Figure 2-1 outlines the logic of the program shown in Figure 1-3. Shown with the program and flowchart is the corresponding pseudocode. Pseudocode is an alternate means of depicting the logic behind a computer program.

Flowcharts.   As you can see from the example, a *program flowchart* consists of geometric symbols and arrows. Each symbol contains an operation the computer must perform, and the arrows show the flow of the program logic (in other words, which operation is to be performed next).

As you have probably already noticed, not all of the symbols have the same shape. The shape of the symbol used depends on the type of operation being performed. The symbols used in this *Guide,* along with their program statement types, are shown in Figure 2-2.

You should note in Figure 2-1 that not every BASIC program statement will necessarily correspond to a flowchart symbol; conversely, not every flowchart symbol corresponds to a BASIC program statement. For example, there is no BASIC program-statement counterpart to the flowcharting "START" symbol. The BASIC program shown actually begins with a REM statement. Also, there is no flowchart symbol for the DATA statement. The flowchart is intended to represent only the flow of program logic. This can be done without specifying actual values for the variables.

You should also note in Figure 2-1 that the flowchart need not contain every detail that will be specified in the program but only those that are important for understanding the logical flow. Thus, the flowchart indicates the output as "Print square," whereas statement 170 of the corresponding program specifies in more detail:

Figure 2-1 Program, flowchart, and pseudocode for computing and printing the squares of several numbers (previously presented in Figure 1-3).

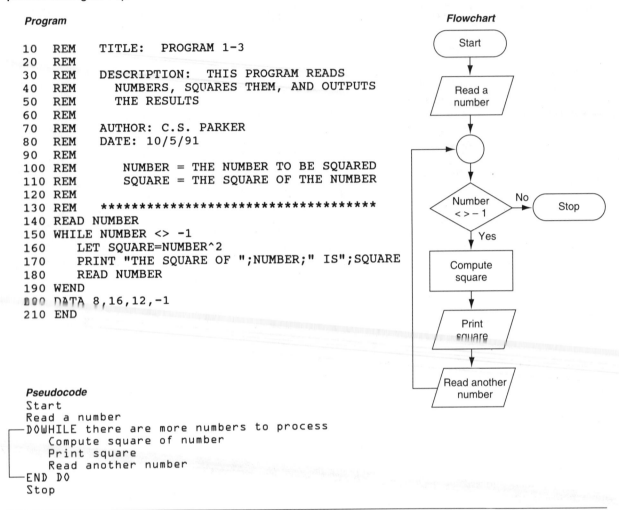

Program

```
10   REM   TITLE:   PROGRAM 1-3
20   REM
30   REM   DESCRIPTION:  THIS PROGRAM READS
40   REM     NUMBERS, SQUARES THEM, AND OUTPUTS
50   REM     THE RESULTS
60   REM
70   REM   AUTHOR: C.S. PARKER
80   REM   DATE: 10/5/91
90   REM
100  REM       NUMBER = THE NUMBER TO BE SQUARED
110  REM       SQUARE = THE SQUARE OF THE NUMBER
120  REM
130  REM   **********************************
140  READ NUMBER
150  WHILE NUMBER <> -1
160      LET SQUARE=NUMBER^2
170      PRINT "THE SQUARE OF ";NUMBER;" IS";SQUARE
180      READ NUMBER
190  WEND
200  DATA 8,16,12,-1
210  END
```

Flowchart

Pseudocode
```
Start
Read a number
DOWHILE there are more numbers to process
    Compute square of number
    Print square
    Read another number
END DO
Stop
```

```
170 PRINT "THE SQUARE OF ";NUMBER;" IS ";SQUARE
```

Pseudocode. Whereas program flowcharts use graphical symbols to depict program logic, *pseudocode* uses English-like statements. Pseudocode is widely considered to be a better tool than flowcharts for designing structured programs. Although it is possible to create unstructured flowcharts, it is virtually impossible to create unstructured pseudocode.

All of the programs, flowcharts, and pseudocode represented in this text reflect a *structured* programming style. This style involves the strict use of three program structures: *sequence, selection,* and *looping* (shown in Figure 2-3). Virtually every programming problem that you encounter can be satisfactorily solved by using some combination of these—and only these—three structures. Note that the flowchart and pseudocode in Figure 2-1 involve a looping structure (DOWHILE) and, within the loop, a sequence of three statements. In a

Symbol	Name	Description	Figure 2-2
			Flowcharting symbols
(stadium shape)	Start/Stop	Used to begin and end every flowchart	
(parallelogram)	Input/Output	Used to represent the READ or INPUT statements on input, PRINT statement on output	
(rectangle)	Assignment	Used to represent the LET statement	
(diamond)	Decision	Used to represent the IF and WHILE statements	
(circle)	Connector	Used to represent the NEXT statement or used to continue the flowchart when running out of room	
(hexagon)	Loop	Used to represent the FOR statement	

DOWHILE structure, the procedure in a loop is performed *while* a condition is true, whereas in a DOUNTIL structure, the procedure in a loop is performed *until* a condition becomes true. Many versions of BASIC do not support the DOUNTIL looping structure, in which the procedure within a loop is always performed *at least once* and the test of the condition is performed at the bottom of the loop. In DOWHILE, by contrast, the loop procedure may not be performed at all (if the condition is initially false) and the test of the condition is performed at the top of the loop.

Just as there are many conventions used to construct flowcharts, so, too, are there many ways to develop pseudocode. The convention used in this text is to capitalize certain keywords, such as those shown in Figure 2-3, and to begin and end the pseudocode with the keywords "Start" and "Stop," respectively. Also, although it is not mandatory, the convention chosen in this *Guide* is to depict pseudocode at a very general level. Most professionals seem to prefer this style because if the pseudocode were too detailed, one might be better off just coding the program. While flowcharts can also be constructed at a general level, we've selected a detailed level here to give you better insight into how each corresponding BASIC program works.

Both flowcharts and pseudocode are useful as design tools for developing programs and, later, as program *documentation* aids. As a design tool, the flow-

Figure 2-3   Flowchart and pseudocode forms of the three fundamental control structures—sequence, selection, and looping.

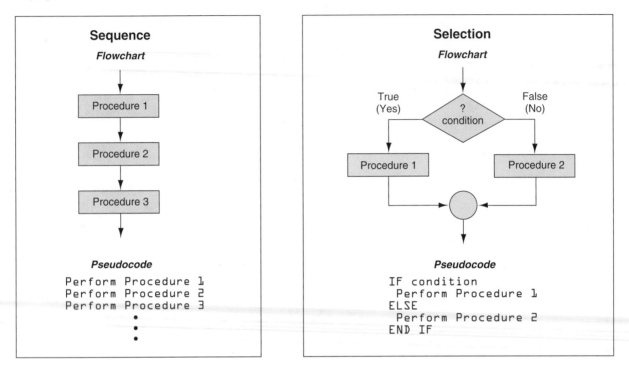

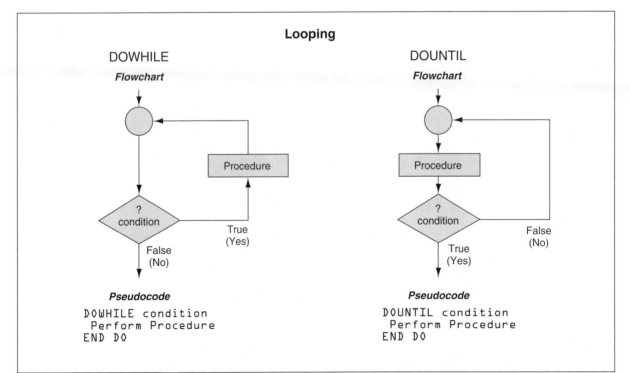

chart or pseudocode lets the programmer "think through" the logical design of programs before writing them. This can be particularly helpful for the same reason a builder of a house consults a floor plan before constructing any individual room. Once a program is written, the flowchart or pseudocode becomes a documentation aid: it generally is easier for others to understand how a program works by studying the flowchart or pseudocode than the program itself. Also, because of their simplicity, flowcharts or pseudocode can often be understood by nonprogrammers.

Some Further Examples

Now that we've covered some of the fundamentals of flowcharting and pseudocode, we'll look at two further examples.

First, let's consider a simple problem involving the selection structure. Team A and Team B, crosstown rivals, played each other in baseball a total of five times during the course of a season. The results were as follows:

Game	Team A Score	Team B Score
1	8	5
2	6	7
3	2	0
4	0	1
5	5	4

Create a flowchart, pseudocode, and, finally, a BASIC program that will output, for each game, the team winning the game. The solution, which involves a simple selection structure within a loop, is shown in Figure 2-4.

As our second example, let's take another look at the problem solved in Figure 1-8 (page 28). There we were required to find all employees in a company who are female, over 40, and work in the accounting department. The associated program, flowchart, and pseudocode are shown in Figure 2-5. Note that the flowchart and pseudocode involve a looping structure and, within the loop, three selection structures. When selection structures are *nested* in pseudocode, as they are in the figure, every IF keyword is paired with an ELSE keyword, and there is an END IF terminating each structure.

Several other examples of flowcharts and pseudocode will be presented in later sections of this *Guide*.

Flowcharting and Pseudocoding Problems*

Instructions: Write a flowchart and pseudocode to do each of the following tasks.

1. Three numbers (no two of which are equal) are to be read by the computer system and assigned to variables A, B, and C, respectively. Determine the

---

*For additional practice, try providing flowchart and pseudocode solutions to the problems described in Programming Problems 3–8 in Section 1 (pages 30–31). If you want to test your knowledge quickly, try Problems 4 and 7 first.

Figure 2-4   Program, flowchart, and pseudocode for solving a simple baseball problem.

Program

```
10   REM    TITLE:  PROGRAM 2-4
20   REM
30   REM    DESCRIPTION:  THIS PROGRAM
40   REM      PICKS GAME WINNERS
50   REM
60   REM    AUTHOR: C.S. PARKER
70   REM    DATE: 10/5/91
80   REM
90   REM    GAME   = THE GAME NUMBER
100  REM    ASCORE = TEAM "A" SCORE
110  REM    BSCORE = TEAM "B" SCORE
120  REM
130  REM ********************************************
140  READ GAME,ASCORE,BSCORE
150  WHILE GAME <> 0
160     REM ASSUME NO GAMES END IN A TIE
170     IF ASCORE > BSCORE THEN PRINT "TEAM A WINS GAME";GAME
                           ELSE PRINT "TEAM B WINS GAME";GAME
180     READ GAME,ASCORE,BSCORE
190  WEND
200  REM ***********DATA STATEMENTS********************
210  DATA 1,8,5
220  DATA 2,6,7
230  DATA 3,2,0
240  DATA 4,0,1
250  DATA 5,5,4
260  DATA 0,0,0
270  REM ********************************************
280  END

RUN
TEAM A WINS GAME 1
TEAM B WINS GAME 2
TEAM A WINS GAME 3
TEAM B WINS GAME 4
TEAM A WINS GAME 5
```

Figure 2-4 *continued*

Pseudocode
```
Start
Read game number and score
DOWHILE there are more scores to process
   IF A's score > B's score
      Print "TEAM A WINS"
   ELSE
      Print "TEAM B WINS"
   END IF
   Read game number and score
END DO
Stop
```

Flowchart

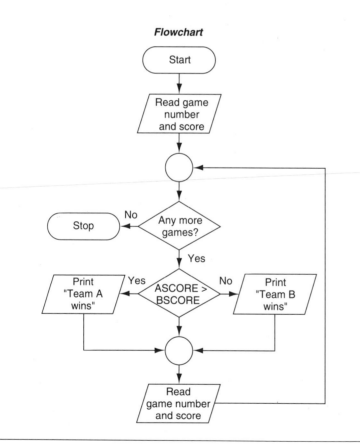

Figure 2-5   Program, flowchart, and pseudocode for solving an employee selection problem (previously presented in Figure 1-8).

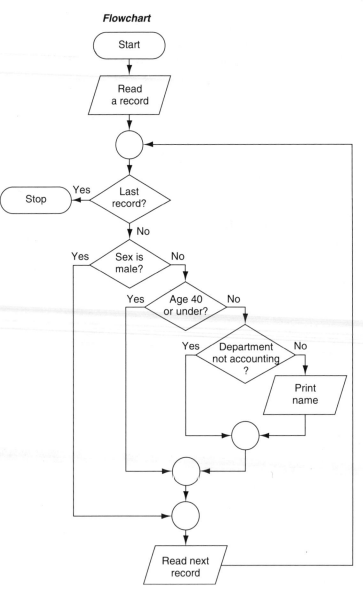

Flowchart

Figure 2-5 *continued*

Program

```
10   REM    TITLE:   PROGRAM 1-8
20   REM
30   REM    DESCRIPTION: THIS PROGRAM SELECTS FROM
40   REM      A FILE ALL FEMALE EMPLOYEES OVER 40
50   REM       WHO WORK IN THE ACCOUNTING DEPARTMENT
60   REM
70   REM    AUTHOR - C.S. PARKER
80   REM    DATE: 10/5/91
90   REM
100  REM    EMPLOYEE$ = EMPLOYEE NAME
110  REM    SEX$       = SEX
120  REM    AGE        = AGE
130  REM    DEPT$      = DEPARTMENT
140  REM
150  REM ***********************************
160  READ EMPLOYEE$,SEX$,AGE,DEPT$
170  WHILE EMPLOYEE$ <> "LAST RECORD"
180      IF SEX$ = "MALE" THEN 220
190      IF AGE <= 40 THEN 220
200      IF DEPT$ <> "ACCOUNTING" THEN 220
210      PRINT EMPLOYEE$
220      READ EMPLOYEE$,SEX$,AGE,DEPT$
230  WEND
240  REM *********DATA STATEMENTS**********
250  DATA "JANE CRIBBS","FEMALE",25,"ACCOUNTING"
260  DATA "PHIL JONES","MALE",45,"ACCOUNTING"
270  DATA "ANNE WELLES","FEMALE",42,"ACCOUNTING"
280  DATA "MARY SMITH","FEMALE",41,"FINANCE"
290  DATA "LAST RECORD","MALE",99,"NONE"
300  REM ***********************************
310  END
```

Pseudocode
```
Start
Read an employee record
DOWHILE there are more records to process
  ┌IF sex is male
  │     Next statement
  │ ELSE
  │     ┌IF age ≤ 40
  │     │    Next statement
  │     │ ELSE
  │     │    ┌IF department < > "ACCOUNTING"
  │     │    │    Next statement
  │     │    │ ELSE
  │     │    │    Print name
  │     │    └END IF
  │     └END IF
  └END IF
   Read next record
END DO
Stop
```

largest, smallest, and middle number. (For example, if A is 3, B is 1, and C is 6, then 6 is the largest, 1 is the smallest, and 3 is the middle number.)

2. The following tax table is used to calculate the tax in a certain state:

Tax Rate Schedules

Table X
(Single Taxpayers)

If the Bottom Line Amount on Your Tax Return Is	Compute Your Tax as Follows:
$0–1,000	2% of the amount
$1,001–10,000	4% of the amount less $100
$10,001–50,000	6% of the amount less $300
Over $50,000	7% of the amount

Use this table to design a procedure to compute taxes due for a list of tax-payers.

3. A state charges the following annual fees for fishing licenses:

	Resident	Nonresident
All species	$10.00	$22.00
All species except trout	$ 7.00	$15.00

Use this table to design a procedure to compute the fee to be charged for each person buying a license. Following are some sample data to test the correctness of your procedure.

Individual	Residency Status	License Wanted
Merlon Biggs	Resident	All species
Alexis Adams	Resident	All species except trout
Arlen Bixby	Nonresident	All species
Al Allen	Nonresident	All species except trout

SECTION 3
EXPANDING ON THE
BASICS OF BASIC

Counting and Summing

Now that we've covered a few fundamentals of how BASIC works, let's tackle a slightly more complicated problem. The example in Figure 3-1, a program to compute and print the average of a group of positive numbers, introduces two of the most fundamental operations in computing: counting and summing. You should observe the "mechanics" of both of these operations very carefully, because they occur in almost every large-scale programming problem.

Three important observations should be made about the program in Figure 3-1:

1. Statements 150 (LET COUNT=0) and 160 (LET SUM=0) establish *explicitly* the beginning values of COUNT and SUM. Establishing beginning values for variables is called *initialization*. Most versions of BASIC will *implicitly* initialize all variables to zero before the program is executed; thus, statements 150 and 160 are usually unnecessary. It is good practice, however, to explicitly initialize certain variables to zero whether or not it is necessary on your computer system. There are two reasons for this practice:

    a. Many programming languages will not automatically initialize variables to zero. This can lead to surprising results if you didn't explicitly initialize, because numbers from someone else's program may be lurking in the storage locations assigned to your variables. Thus, your variables will assume these arbitrary values.

    b. When you initialize explicitly, the intent of your program becomes more evident. In other words, initialization is good documentation.

    Only the variables COUNT and SUM require initialization to zero in this program. These are the variables for which the computer needs to "look up" the values on the right-hand side of the assignment symbol (=) in lines 190 and 200, respectively. The variables NUMBER and AVERAGE don't have to be initialized, since they never appear on the right-hand side of an assignment symbol before the computer has explicitly assigned them a value.

2. Statement 190 (LET COUNT = COUNT + 1) *counts* the number of numbers in the list. COUNT is initially assigned a value of zero. Each time a positive number is read into storage for NUMBER (so that the "NUMBER <> −1" condition is true in line 180 of the program), 1 is added to the current value of COUNT. Because only one number can be assigned to COUNT at any time, the previous value of COUNT is destroyed and lost forever.

3. Statement 200 (LET SUM = SUM + NUMBER) *sums* the numbers in the list. As with COUNT, SUM is initially zero. Each time statement 200 is executed, the current value of NUMBER is added to the current value of SUM. Thus, SUM can be seen as a "running total," as indicated in the following table:

Figure 3-1   Computing the average of several numbers.

Program

```
10  REM    TITLE:   PROGRAM 3-1
20  REM
30  REM    DESCRIPTION: THIS PROGRAM COMPUTES AND OUTPUTS
40  REM       THE AVERAGE OF SEVERAL POSITIVE NUMBERS
50  REM
60  REM    AUTHOR: C.S. PARKER
70  REM    DATE: 10/5/91
80  REM
90  REM    COUNT   = COUNT VARIABLE
100 REM    SUM     = SUM VARIABLE
110 REM    NUMBER  = A NUMBER IN THE LIST
120 REM    AVERAGE = AVERAGE OF ALL NUMBERS
130 REM
140 REM  ******************************
150 LET COUNT = 0
160 LET SUM = 0
170 READ NUMBER
180 WHILE NUMBER <> -1
190    LET COUNT = COUNT + 1
200    LET SUM = SUM + NUMBER
210    READ NUMBER
220 WEND
230 LET AVERAGE = SUM / COUNT
240 PRINT "AVERAGE IS";AVERAGE
250 DATA 7,23,33,15,42,-1
260 END

RUN
AVERAGE IS 24
```

Pseudocode
```
Start
Initialize count and sum
Read a number
DOWHILE there are more numbers to process
    Increment counter by 1
    Add number to sum
    Read next number
END DO
Compute average
Print average
Stop
```

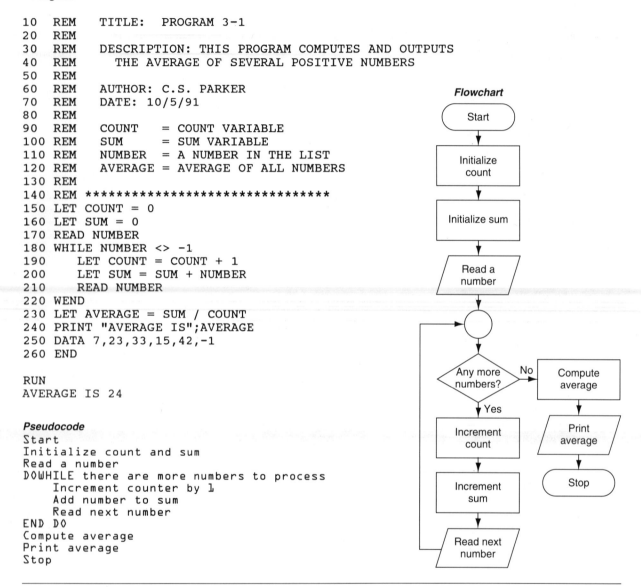

Flowchart

When the Value of NUMBER Is	Statement 200 Does the Following
7	Adds 7 to the initial sum, 0, producing SUM = 7
23	Adds 23 to 7, producing SUM = 30
33	Adds 33 to 30, producing SUM = 63
15	Adds 15 to 63, producing SUM = 78
42	Adds 42 to 78, producing SUM = 120
−1	Statement 200 is not executed when NUMBER = −1

The INPUT Statement

The INPUT statement is one of the most useful statements in the BASIC language. It permits the program user to operate in a *conversational (interactive) mode* with the computer system. In other words, during the course of executing a program, the computer system asks the user for a response, and the user answers; then, based on the response given, the computer system asks the user for a response to another question, and so forth. The format of the INPUT statement is as follows:

> Line # INPUT list of variables (separated by commas)

Figure 3-2 shows the program in Figure 3-1 rewritten with the INPUT statement. You should carefully note the following:

1. The READ statement in Figure 3-1 has been changed to an INPUT statement in Figure 3-2. With the READ statement, all data to be assigned to NUMBER are placed in an associated DATA statement; remember, READ and DATA statements are always used together. When we use INPUT NUMBER, no corresponding DATA statement is employed. Instead we supply data to the computer system as the program is running.
2. Data are supplied to the computer system as follows. Whenever an INPUT statement is encountered, a "?" is output by the system, and processing temporarily halts. At this point, we must enter as many data values as there are variables appearing after the word INPUT in the program. These values must be separated by commas. After we depress the Enter key, the system will assign the values to their corresponding variables and resume processing. If the same or another INPUT statement is encountered, the system will again respond with a question mark and await more input from the user.
3. In lines 170 and 220, just before the INPUT statements, are PRINT statements that provide instructions for the user of the program. When writing programs that include INPUT statements, it is always a good idea to include such a *prompting* PRINT statement before each INPUT so that the user will know both how to enter data into the computer and how to stop the program.

The major advantage of the INPUT statement over READ is that the user and computer system are involved in a dynamic dialog. In many cases, the user may not know the inputs in advance, since they depend on actions taken by the computer.

The STOP Statement

Execution of a STOP statement in a program causes the program to halt execution, often by immediate transfer to the END statement. The STOP statement has the following format:

> Line # STOP

Figure 3-2   Program in Figure 3-1 rewritten with the INPUT statement.

```
10  REM     TITLE:   PROGRAM 3-2
20  REM
30  REM     DESCRIPTION: THIS PROGRAM COMPUTES AND OUTPUTS
40  REM        THE AVERAGE OF SEVERAL POSITIVE NUMBERS
50  REM
60  REM     AUTHOR: C.S. PARKER
70  REM     DATE: 10/5/91
80  REM
90  REM     COUNT   = COUNT VARIABLE
100 REM     SUM     = SUM VARIABLE
110 REM     NUMBER  = A NUMBER IN THE LIST
120 REM     AVERAGE = AVERAGE OF ALL NUMBERS
130 REM
140 REM *****************************
150 LET COUNT = 0
160 LET SUM = 0
170 PRINT "ENTER A POSITIVE NUMBER (OR -1 TO STOP)"
180 INPUT NUMBER
190 WHILE NUMBER <> -1
200     LET COUNT = COUNT + 1
210     LET SUM = SUM + NUMBER
220     PRINT "ENTER A POSITIVE NUMBER (OR -1 TO STOP)"
230     INPUT NUMBER
240 WEND
250 LET AVERAGE = SUM / COUNT
260 PRINT "AVERAGE IS";AVERAGE
270 DATA 7,23,33,15,42,-1
280 END
```

— Input statements

```
RUN
ENTER A POSITIVE NUMBER (OR -1 TO STOP)
? 7
ENTER A POSITIVE NUMBER (OR -1 TO STOP)
? 23
ENTER A POSITIVE NUMBER (OR -1 TO STOP)
? 33
ENTER A POSITIVE NUMBER (OR -1 TO STOP)
? 15
ENTER A POSITIVE NUMBER (OR -1 TO STOP)
? 42
ENTER A POSITIVE NUMBER (OR -1 TO STOP)
? -1
AVERAGE IS 24
```

Later, in Figures 3-6 and 3-9, you will see how the STOP statement works. In Figure 3-6, for instance, as soon as the STOP statement is executed, the message

```
Break in 200
```

is output and the program terminates immediately. At this point, BASIC's "Ok" prompt will appear on the screen, indicating that you are free to next do what you like.

FOR and NEXT Statements

The FOR and NEXT statements, which allow the programmer to loop (repeat a program section) automatically, are among the most important statements in BASIC. For example, consider the short program given in Figure 3-3.

The FOR and NEXT statements form a "sandwich," or loop. All statements inside the loop are executed the number of times determined in the FOR statement. (Note that these statements are indented, making the program easier to read.) In Figure 3-3, I is first set equal to 1. Then everything inside the loop (that is, statement 20) is executed; I is then set equal to 2 and statement 20 is executed again; and so forth. After I is set equal to 5 and the loop is executed for the fifth time, control passes to the statement that immediately follows the NEXT statement (in other words, statement 40).

FOR and NEXT statements are always used together. They physically establish the beginning and end of the loop. Like READ and DATA, one statement makes absolutely no sense unless the other is present. The format of these statements is:

Line # FOR loop-variable = $\left\{ \begin{array}{c} \text{Beginning} \\ \text{value} \end{array} \right\}$ TO $\left\{ \begin{array}{c} \text{Ending} \\ \text{value} \end{array} \right\}$ STEP increment

    .
    .
    .

Line # NEXT loop-variable

The use of the loop variable, beginning value, ending value, and increment will now be explained.

The variable I in the program of Figure 3-3 is an example of a *loop variable*. Note carefully that the chosen loop variable (which can be any acceptable BASIC numeric variable) must be included in both the FOR statement and its associated NEXT statement, as indicated in the figure.

In Figure 3-3, it was implicitly assumed that the loop variable was to be incremented by 1 each time the loop was executed. The increment could also have been explicitly declared in a STEP clause:

```
10 FOR I=1 TO 5 STEP 1
```

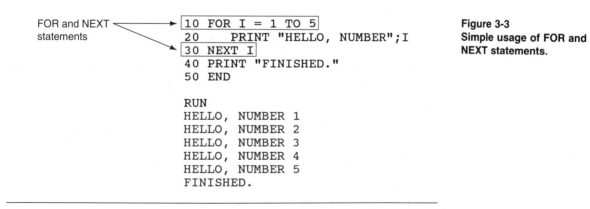

FOR and NEXT statements

```
10 FOR I = 1 TO 5
20      PRINT "HELLO, NUMBER";I
30 NEXT I
40 PRINT "FINISHED."
50 END

RUN
HELLO, NUMBER 1
HELLO, NUMBER 2
HELLO, NUMBER 3
HELLO, NUMBER 4
HELLO, NUMBER 5
FINISHED.
```

Figure 3-3
Simple usage of FOR and NEXT statements.

The results produced would be the same. If, on the other hand, we rewrote line 10 as

```
10 FOR I=1 TO 5 STEP 3
```

and ran the program, the computer system would respond

```
HELLO, NUMBER 1
HELLO, NUMBER 4
FINISHED.
```

Since the next possible incremented value, 7, exceeds the ending value of 5, the computer doesn't execute the loop for a third time but passes control to statement 40.

It is also possible to let the loop variable work "backwards." For example, if we changed line 10 of Figure 3-3 to read

```
10 FOR I=5 TO 1 STEP -1
```

we would obtain

```
HELLO, NUMBER 5
HELLO, NUMBER 4
HELLO, NUMBER 3
HELLO, NUMBER 2
HELLO, NUMBER 1
FINISHED.
```

BASIC also allows programmers to use variables in FOR and NEXT statements. For example, the following sequence is also acceptable:

```
30 FOR Z=J TO K STEP L
              .
              .
              .
70 NEXT Z
```

If J = 2, K = 10, and L = 3, the loop will be performed 3 times, with Z taking on values of 2, 5, and 8 as the loop is executed.

Let's now consider a more comprehensive example to further explore the concept of looping. Consider again the "averages" problem solved in Figure 3-1 (page 44). How can we solve this problem using FOR/NEXT loops? The flowchart and program solution appear in Figure 3-4.

Note, in comparing the two programs, that because the number of times the FOR/NEXT loop is executed is predetermined before looping begins, no trailer value is needed in the DATA statement. Also note that FOR/NEXT logic can be simulated in pseudocode through a DOWHILE looping structure. This requires a separate Set instruction before the loop to initialize the counter and a separate Add instruction at the end of the loop to increment the counter.

Figure 3-4   Solution to the problem in Figure 3-1 using loops.

Program

```
10   REM    TITLE:   PROGRAM 3-4
20   REM
30   REM    DESCRIPTION: THIS PROGRAM COMPUTES AND OUTPUTS
40   REM       THE AVERAGE OF SEVERAL POSITIVE NUMBERS
50   REM
60   REM    AUTHOR: C.S. PARKER
70   REM    DATE: 10/5/91
80   REM
90   REM    I       = LOOP VARIABLE
100  REM    SUM     = SUM VARIABLE
110  REM    NUMBER  = A NUMBER IN THE LIST
120  REM    AVERAGE = AVERAGE OF ALL NUMBERS
130  REM    TOTAL   = THE NUMBER OF NUMBERS
140  REM
150  REM ******************************
160  LET SUM = 0
170  READ TOTAL
180  FOR I = 1 TO TOTAL
190     READ NUMBER
200     LET SUM = SUM + NUMBER
210  NEXT I
220  LET AVERAGE = SUM / TOTAL
230  PRINT "AVERAGE IS";AVERAGE
240  DATA 5
250  DATA 7,23,33,15,42
260  END

RUN
AVERAGE IS 24
```

Pseudocode
```
Start
Initialize sum to zero
Read the list size
Set counter to 1
DOWHILE counter ≤ list size
   Read a number
   Add number to sum
   Add 1 to counter
END DO
Compute average
Print average
Stop
```

Flowchart

Finally, loops within loops, or *nested loops,* are allowed. Observe the short program below.

```
10 FOR I=1 TO 3
20    FOR J=1 TO 2
30       PRINT I;J
40    NEXT J
50 NEXT I
60 END
RUN
 1    1
 1    2
 2    1
 2    2
 3    1
 3    2
 ↑    ↑
 Ⓘ    Ⓙ
```

The program executes the PRINT statement a total of $3 * 2 = 6$ times. The outer-loop variable (I) varies the slowest, the inner-loop variable (J) varies the fastest.

In writing nested-loop programs, it is always important to enclose the inner loop entirely within the outer loop. Thus, a program segment such as the one following,

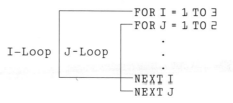

```
         ┌──────FOR I = 1 TO 3
         │  ┌───FOR J = 1 TO 2
         │  │      .
I-Loop   J-Loop    .
         │  │      .
         │  └───NEXT I
         └──────NEXT J
```

would not work because the loops cross rather than nest.

Subroutines

BASIC *subroutines* are partial programs, or subprograms, that are contained within a BASIC program (called the *main program*). They are particularly effective when a series of statements in a program is to be performed numerous times or when a program is long and requires rigorous organization.

Subroutines enable programs to be organized in a modular, top-down fashion, as shown in the structure chart in Figure 3-5. The main part of the program, which is the topmost module, performs control functions. The modules at the lower levels do the actual work. Anyone contemplating a career as a programmer is well advised to practice as much as possible writing programs in the modular, top-down fashion suggested by subroutines.

Each independent task should be done in a separate subroutine, making the main program logic much easier to follow. Such a modular programming style

Figure 3-5 Structure charts.
This technique subdivides a program into individual modules, each of which represents a well-defined processing task. The modules are then arranged hierarchically in a top-down fashion, as illustrated here for a payroll application.

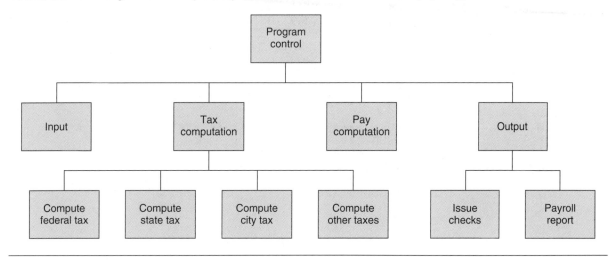

allows new programmers hired by a company to understand more quickly how existing programs work. It also makes debugging easier, since each subroutine can be tested independently with dummy variables.

Although the programs in the *Guide* are short enough that they are perhaps clearer in some cases without the use of subroutines, commercial-level programs usually require strict adherence to modularity. Unless programs that consist of thousands of lines of code are hierarchically organized into independent parts, as suggested in Figure 3-5, they become cluttered, tangled masses.

GOSUB and RETURN.   Subroutines introduce two new statements, GOSUB and RETURN, which have the following formats:

```
Line # GOSUB line-number
 .
 .
 .
Line # RETURN
```

The GOSUB statement causes immediate branching to the first statement in the subroutine. The RETURN statement causes branching back to the main program, to the statement that immediately follows the invoking GOSUB (that is, the GOSUB that caused the branching). Subroutines can also be nested.

An example of a program that uses subroutines and the output of this program are given in Figure 3-6. Figure 3-7 shows a structure chart for this program.

Note the use of the STOP statement in line 200. This statement is necessary so that, when the looping in lines 150 through 190 is finished, the program terminates immediately. If the STOP statement were taken out, the subroutines would be executed one more time between finishing the loop and reaching the END statement.

Figure 3-6
Use of subroutines to solve the problem originally presented in Figure 1-6.

```
10   REM    TITLE: PROGRAM 3-6
20   REM
30   REM    READS A LIST OF NUMBERS
40   REM       AND TELLS WHETHER EACH NUMBER IS
50   REM       POSITIVE OR NEGATIVE
60   REM
70   REM    AUTHOR: C.S. PARKER
80   REM    DATE: 10/5/91
90   REM
100  REM    NUMBER = A POSITIVE OR NEGATIVE NUMBER
110  REM    SIGN$  = SIGN OF THE NUMBER
120  REM
130  REM    *************************************
140  GOSUB 220
150  WHILE NUMBER <> 0
160      GOSUB 250
170      GOSUB 280            ◄─── Main part of program
180      GOSUB 220
190  WEND
200  STOP
210  REM
220  REM SUBROUTINE FOR INPUT
230      READ NUMBER
240  RETURN
250  REM SUBROUTINE TO FIGURE NUMBER'S SIGN
260      IF NUMBER < 0 THEN SIGN$ = "NEGATIVE"
                       ELSE SIGN$ = "POSITIVE"     ◄─── Subroutines
270  RETURN
280  REM SUBROUTINE FOR OUTPUT
290      PRINT NUMBER; "IS ";SIGN$
300  RETURN
310  REM
320  DATA 8,-16,-65,12,0
330  END

RUN
  8 IS POSITIVE
-16 IS NEGATIVE
-65 IS NEGATIVE
 12 IS POSITIVE
```

ON . . . GOSUB.   Subroutines can also be employed effectively in a *case structure* by using the ON . . . GOSUB statement. This statement has the format:

> Line # ON case-variable GOSUB line-number, line-number, . . .

A *case variable* is one that has values such as 1, 2, 3, and so forth that correspond to special situations, or "cases," that must be processed. If the case variable is equal to 1, the computer branches to the first line number after the GOSUB; if the case variable is equal to 2, it branches to the second line number; and so on. The case structure made possible by BASIC's ON . . . GOSUB is ideal for menu-selection programs as well as the Solved Review Problem that immediately follows in the next section. The case structure is a special case of a nested IF-THEN-ELSE, as shown in Figure 3-8.

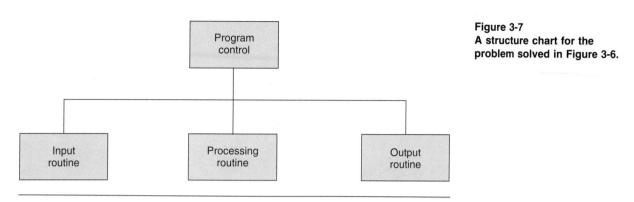

**Figure 3-7
A structure chart for the
problem solved in Figure 3-6.**

Figure 3-8 A case structure.
A case structure is a special case of a nested IF-THEN-ELSE structure. For instance, if the case-variable, TYPE, has a value of 1, Routine-1 is performed; if it has a value of 2, Routine-2 is performed, and so on.

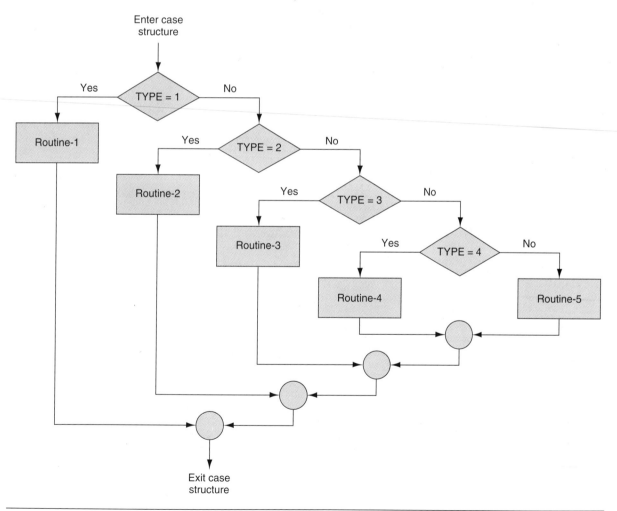

Figure 3-9   An interactive program to determine auto rental charges.

```
10   REM    TITLE:  PROGRAM 3-9
20   REM
30   REM    DESCRIPTION: THIS PROGRAM COMPUTES THE CHARGES
40   REM        DUE ON RENTED AUTOMOBILES
50   REM
60   REM    AUTHOR: C.S. PARKER
70   REM    DATE: 10/5/91
80   REM
90   REM
100  REM    TYPE   = CAR TYPE (1=COMPACT)
110  REM                      (2=INTERMEDIATE)
120  REM                      (3=LARGE)
130  REM    CUSTOMER$ = CUSTOMER NAME
140  REM    DAYS      = DAYS CAR HELD
150  REM    MILES     = MILES TRAVELED
160  REM    CHARGE    = CHARGE FOR CUSTOMER
170  REM
180  REM ***************************************
190  PRINT "ENTER CUSTOMER NAME"
200  PRINT "  NOTE: ENTER GOODBYE TO STOP PROGRAM"
210  INPUT CUSTOMER$
220  WHILE CUSTOMER$ <> "GOODBYE"
230      PRINT "ENTER DAYS CAR HELD, MILES TRAVELED, AND CAR TYPE"
240      PRINT "  NOTE: 1=COMPACT  2=INTERMEDIATE  3=LARGE"
250      INPUT DAYS,MILES,TYPE
260      IF NOT (TYPE = 1 OR TYPE = 2 OR TYPE = 3) THEN TYPE = 4
270      ON TYPE GOSUB 350,400,450,490
280      PRINT "ENTER CUSTOMER NAME"
290      PRINT "  NOTE: ENTER GOODBYE TO STOP PROGRAM"
300      INPUT CUSTOMER$
310  WEND
320  STOP
330  REM **************SUBROUTINES*************************
340  REM COMPACT CAR CALCULATIONS
350      CHARGE = .15 * MILES + 10 * DAYS
360      PRINT CUSTOMER$;"     $";CHARGE
370      PRINT
380      RETURN
390  REM INTERMEDIATE CAR CALCULATIONS
400      CHARGE = .18 * MILES + 20 * DAYS
410      PRINT CUSTOMER$;"     $";CHARGE
420      PRINT
430      RETURN
440  REM LARGE CAR CALCULATIONS
450      CHARGE = .22 * MILES + 30 * DAYS
460      PRINT CUSTOMER$;"     $";CHARGE
470      PRINT
480      RETURN
490  REM ERROR ROUTINE
500      PRINT "YOU HAVE ENTERED AN INVALID CAR TYPE--TRY AGAIN"
510      RETURN
520  REM ***************************************************
530  END
```

Figure 3-9 *continued*

```
RUN
ENTER CUSTOMER NAME
   NOTE: ENTER GOODBYE TO STOP PROGRAM
?JONES
ENTER DAYS CAR HELD, MILES TRAVELED, AND CAR TYPE
   NOTE: 1=COMPACT   2=INTERMEDIATE   3=LARGE
?6,500,3
        $ 290

ENTER CUSTOMER NAME
   NOTE: ENTER GOODBYE TO STOP PROGRAM
?SMITH
ENTER DAYS CAR HELD, MILES TRAVELED, AND CAR TYPE
   NOTE: 1=COMPACT   2=INTERMEDIATE   3=LARGE
?17,3000,1
        $ 620

ENTER CUSTOMER NAME
   NOTE: ENTER GOODBYE TO STOP PROGRAM
?BAKER
ENTER DAYS CAR HELD, MILES TRAVELED, AND CAR TYPE
   NOTE: 1=COMPACT   2=INTERMEDIATE   3=LARGE
?8,250,6
YOU HAVE ENTERED AN INVALID CAR TYPE--TRY AGAIN
ENTER DAYS CAR HELD, MILES TRAVELED, AND CAR TYPE
   NOTE: 1=COMPACT   2=INTERMEDIATE   3=LARGE
?8,250,2
        $ 205

ENTER CUSTOMER NAME
   NOTE: ENTER GOODBYE TO STOP PROGRAM
?WILLIAMS
ENTER DAYS CAR HELD, MILES TRAVELED, AND CAR TYPE
   NOTE: 1=COMPACT   2=INTERMEDIATE   3=LARGE
?4,1000,2
          $ 260

ENTER CUSTOMER NAME
   NOTE: ENTER GOODBYE TO STOP PROGRAM
?WINSTON
ENTER DAYS CAR HELD, MILES TRAVELED, AND CAR TYPE
   NOTE: 1=COMPACT   2=INTERMEDIATE   3=LARGE
?3,500,3
          $ 200

ENTER CUSTOMER NAME
   NOTE: ENTER GOODBYE TO STOP PROGRAM
?GOODBYE
```

Solved Review Problem

An auto rental company rents three types of cars at the following rates:

Car Type	Fixed Cost per Day	Cost per Mile
Compact	$10	$0.15
Intermediate	$20	$0.18
Large	$30	$0.22

Thus, for example, a person renting a compact car for 3 days and driving 100 miles would be charged $10 * 3 + .15 * 100 = \$45$.

Write an interactive BASIC program that will accept

☐ Customer name   ☐ Number of days car held

☐ Car type   ☐ Miles traveled

as input. It should output the charge for each customer. Use the sample data in the following table to test your program.

Customer Name	Car Type	Days Held	Miles Traveled
Jones	Large	6	500
Smith	Compact	17	3,000
Baker	Intermediate	8	250
Williams	Intermediate	4	1,000
Winston	Large	3	500

The solution to this problem is provided in Figure 3-9 (pages 54 and 55). You should note that the program will terminate if the user types in "GOODBYE" when asked to supply a customer name.

In Figure 3-9, pay particular attention to the error-trapping feature of the program. If the user keys in any car type other than TYPE 1, 2, or 3, line 260 sets TYPE = 4. Then, in line 270, the program is directed to a subroutine that processes the error.

Exercises

Instructions: Provide an answer to each of the following questions.

1. Identify the syntax errors, if any, in the following BASIC statements:

    a. 10 FOR I=6 TO 1 STEP 2
    b. 10 INPUT N$,A,A1
    c. 10 INPUT T=1, T=2, T=3
    d. 15 IF N$="PHONY" THEN 25
    e. 10 FOR I=-5 TO 5
    f. 10 FOR K=3 TO A STEP 2

2. Consider the following FOR/NEXT loop:

```
10 FOR I=A TO B STEP C
          .
          .
          .
20 NEXT I
```

How many times will this loop execute if

a.　A=1, B=7, and C=1?　　c.　A=5, B=17, and C=3?
b.　A=1, B=7, and C=2?　　d.　A=5, B=1, and C=−1?

3.　Consider the following program:

```
10 FOR I=1 TO 5
20 FOR J=3 TO 7
30 A=I*J
40 NEXT J
50 NEXT I
```

a.　What is the first value assigned to A?
b.　What is the value of A at the end of the program?
c.　What is the value of A the 8th time statement 30 is executed?
d.　What is the value of A the 12th time statement 30 is executed?
e.　How many times will line 30 be executed?

Programming Problems

Instructions: Write a BASIC program to do each of the following tasks.

1.　Read a list of positive numbers, sum all of the numbers greater than 10 in the list, and output that sum. Use the following list of numbers to check your program:

$$32, 45, 6, 87, 4, 5, 17, 25$$

2.　Sum all even numbers from 1 to 100 and output the square root of that sum. [*Hint:* The square root of any number X is $X^{1/2}$.]
3.　Read a list of positive numbers, find the average of all numbers between 10 and 20 (inclusive) in the list, and output the average. Use the list of numbers given in Programming Problem 1 to check your results.
4.　Write a program that will read in the 10 values

$$-6, 8, 65, 4, 8, -21, 2, 46, -12, 42$$

and identify the highest and lowest number. [*Hint:* Declare the first number in the list as both the highest and lowest value in the list. Then let each of the remaining nine numbers "get a shot" at competing for highest or lowest value. As each number is read, check it against the current high value and low value.]
5.　The following data show the weather in a city on 10 successive days: Sunny, Cloudy, Rainy, Sunny, Sunny, Cloudy, Sunny, Sunny, Rainy, Cloudy.

　　Write a program to read these 10 weather observations and then count and output the number of sunny days.

6. Use FOR/NEXT loops to compute the following sums (S):

$$S = 1 + 2 + 3 + 4 + \cdots + 10$$
$$S = 3 + 6 + 9 + 12 + \cdots + 30$$
$$S = 1 + 1/2 + 1/3 + 1/4 + \cdots + 1/1000$$

7. Write a program to convert several temperatures from Fahrenheit (F) to centigrade (C). Use the INPUT statement to supply each Fahrenheit temperature to the computer system for conversion. The following formula can be used to make the conversion:

```
C=(5/9)*(F-32)
```

Use a trailer value, such as 9999 degrees, to stop your program.

8. The cost of sending a telegram is $2.80 for the first 20 (or fewer) words and 10 cents for each additional word. Write a program that will find the cost of a telegram after you have entered the number of words as input at a keyboard.

9. The population growth rate in a city has been projected at 5 percent per year for the next 10 years. The current population in the city is 31,840 residents. Write a program to find the population 10 years from now.

10. ABC Company has the following accounts receivable data:

Customer Name	Previous Balance	Payments	New Purchases
Clara Bronson	$700	$500	$300
Lon Brooks	100	100	0
Louise Chaplin	0	0	100
Jack Davies	50	0	0
Emil Murray	600	600	200
Tom Swanson	300	100	50
Lucy Allen	500	500	80

Write a subroutine that computes the new balance for each customer. Assume that unpaid portions of previous balances are assessed a 2 percent finance charge each month. The main part of your program should perform all the input/output functions necessary to support and supplement the subroutine.

11. Students in a class have taken a ten-question true/false exam. Below are the results and the correct answers:

Student ID Number	Questions									
	1	2	3	4	5	6	7	8	9	10
40033	F	T	F	F	T	F	F	F	T	T
40055	F	F	F	T	T	F	T	F	T	T
40058	F	T	F	T	F	F	T	F	F	T
40062	F	T	T	T	T	F	T	T	T	F
40066	T	T	F	T	T	F	T	F	F	T
40083	T	T	F	F	T	T	T	F	T	T
Correct answers	T	T	T	T	T	T	T	T	T	T

Score each exam. Assume grades are to be recorded as the percentage of right answers—in other words, 0, 10, 20, . . ., 100 are possible exam scores.

SECTION 4
FORMATTED PRINTING

Spacing Output

Producing neatly formatted output is one of the prized skills of computer programming. A sloppy-looking report, even though it contains accurate information, often is not read. Readers of reports generally are favorably inclined toward well-presented output.

So far we have learned two formatting vehicles to use with the PRINT statement:

1.   The semicolon. This generally leaves a space or two between printed items.*
     When it is the last character in the PRINT statement, it forces the next output
     from the computer system to begin on the same line.
2.   The "blank" PRINT statement. This is used to produce blank output lines.

There are three other techniques discussed in this section that will aid in formatting output:

1.   The comma (,).
2.   The TAB function.
3.   The PRINT USING statement.

Comma Print Control

The comma works in a manner somewhat similar to the semicolon, except that

1.   It produces more space between the output data items.
2.   The items are printed at fixed tab stops.

The fixed tab stops define so-called *print zones*. If you are on an output device that provides 80 characters per line, the zones might be fixed as follows:

Zone 1	Zone 2	Zone 3	Zone 4	Zone 5
Columns	Columns	Columns	Columns	Columns
1–14	15–28	29–42	43–56	57–80

In any case, you should check your output device to find out where the zones begin and end. With the zones just mentioned, the use of commas in a PRINT statement would have the effect shown in Figure 4-1, which features a simple program that inputs data and merely outputs the same data into zones. Positive numbers printed in a zone are preceded by a blank space, negative numbers by a minus sign.

---

*The exception is that no spaces are provided between two strings separated by a semicolon (unless, of course, spaces appear within the string).

Figure 4-1
Use of comma in PRINT for spacing.
This simple program reads in names of people along with associated pay rates and gross pay. This information is then output into print zones.

```
10   REM    TITLE:   PROGRAM 4-1
20   REM
30   REM    DESCRIPTION: THIS PROGRAM LISTS PAY
40   REM        RATES AND GROSS PAY OF EMPLOYEES
50   REM
60   REM    AUTHOR: C.S. PARKER
70   REM    DATE: 10/5/91
80   REM
90   REM    EMPLOYEE$  = EMPLOYEE NAME
100  REM    RATE       = PAY RATE
110  REM    GROSS      = GROSS PAY
120  REM    I          = LOOP VARIABLE
130  REM
140  REM  ****************************************
150  PRINT "NAME","PAY RATE","GROSS PAY"
160  PRINT
170  FOR I = 1 TO 3
180      READ EMPLOYEE$,RATE,GROSS
190      PRINT EMPLOYEE$,RATE,GROSS
200  NEXT I
210  DATA "JOHN DOE",6.30,200.15
220  DATA "MARY SMITH",7.20,316.40
230  DATA "ANN JONES",5.00,80.00
240  END
```

Line 190 — Print statement with zone spacing

```
RUN
NAME            PAY RATE        GROSS PAY

JOHN DOE        6.3             200.15
MARY SMITH      7.2             316.4
ANN JONES       5               80
```

| Zone 1 | Zone 2 | Zone 3 |

There are two other interesting features to note about the use of the comma for spacing in a PRINT statement:

1. If the number of items to be output in a PRINT statement is too large to fit on one line of the output device used, a "wraparound" effect will occur; for example:

```
10 FOR I=1 TO 12
20 PRINT I,
30 NEXT I
40 END
RUN
 1          2          3          4          5
 6          7          8          9          10
 11         12
```

Only five data items are printed per line because only five print zones are available on the output device used. If we tried running this program on a different output device, say, one with six zones, we would get six numbers per line.

2. If a particular data item is too large to occupy a single print zone, it will "overflow" into subsequent zones; for example:

```
10 PRINT "TODAY IS MAY 16, 1992","HELLO"
20 END
RUN
TODAY IS MAY 16, 1992    HELLO
```

Begins in zone 1

Begins in zone 3 (because the first literal overflowed into zone 2)

The TAB Function

The TAB function of BASIC permits us to "tab" over to any column to start printing. Thus, with the TAB function we don't have to begin printing at a zone boundary.

The following self-explanatory example will clarify how the TAB function is used in BASIC:

```
10 PRINT TAB(10);"HELLO"
20 PRINT TAB(15);"HELLO AGAIN"
30 PRINT TAB(20);"HELLO FOR A THIRD TIME"
40 END
RUN
          HELLO
               HELLO AGAIN
                    HELLO FOR A THIRD TIME
```

Starts in column 20

Starts in column 15

Starts in column 10

Note that there must be no space between the word TAB in a statement and the opening parenthesis.

It is possible to use several TAB functions on one line. You can also specify tabbing for a single, long output line that spans two PRINT statements. For example:

```
10 PRINT "PART NUMBER";TAB(20);"NAME";TAB(30);
20 PRINT "AMOUNT IN STOCK";TAB(50);"UNIT PRICE"
30 END
RUN
PART NUMBER        NAME      AMOUNT IN STOCK      UNIT PRICE
```

Column 1   Column 20 Column 30   Column 50

Remember, the semicolon at the end of a PRINT statement (see line 10) will keep the output device on the same line.

In many versions of BASIC, you can use variable names as tab stops; for example:

```
10 F=25
20 PRINT TAB(F);"GOODBYE"
30 END
RUN
```

                                        GOODBYE
                                        ↑
                                        Column 25

The PRINT USING Statement

The PRINT USING statement is the most powerful instruction in BASIC for formatted printing. The syntax of this statement varies considerably from system to system; however, the one presented here and in the examples to follow is used widely:

> Line # PRINT USING output-image-variable;
> list of variables (separated by commas)

A program employing the PRINT USING statement appears in Figure 4-2. This program reads in names (EMPLOYEE$), pay rates (RATE), and hours worked (HOURS). It then computes and sums the amounts earned (AMOUNT=RATE*HOURS). You should examine this example carefully before reading further.

The program uses two PRINT USING statements. Each PRINT USING statement refers to a variable that specifies how to format, or *image*, the output when the PRINT USING is executed. The program in Figure 4-2 contains two such *output-image variables:* A$ and B$. The PRINT USING statement in line 260 references A$, containing the output images of variables EMPLOYEE$, HOURS, and AMOUNT. Similarly, statement 280 references B$, containing the image of variable TOTAL. For both A$ and B$, the associated output image appears between quotation marks (see lines 190 and 200, respectively).

PRINT USING output images are formatted according to the following rules.

Numeric Variables.   All numeric variable values are placed in the areas occupied by the pound (number) signs (#) of their associated output images, in the order in which the variable names appear in the PRINT USING. If the variable value contains a decimal point, you can specify where it must appear and the number of digits to the left and right of it. For example, an image such as

$$\#\#\#\#\#.\#\#$$

specifies that 1245.06 be printed as

    ƀ1245.06   (ƀ represents a blank space)

In many versions of BASIC, commas can also be automatically placed into numeric values. For example, an image such as

Figure 4-2 Use of PRINT USING statement.

```
10   REM    TITLE: PROGRAM 4-2
20   REM
30   REM    DESCRIPTION: THIS PROGRAM COMPUTES EMPLOYEE PAY
40   REM
50   REM    AUTHOR: C.S. PARKER
60   REM    DATE: 10/5/91
70   REM
80   REM    EMPLOYEE$    = EMPLOYEE NAME
90   REM    HOURS        = HOURS WORKED
100  REM    RATE         = PAY RATE
110  REM    AMOUNT       = AMOUNT EARNED BY EMPLOYEE
120  REM    TOTAL        = SUM OF ALL AMOUNTS EARNED
130  REM    I            = LOOP VARIABLE
140  REM    A$,B$        = OUTPUT-IMAGE VARIABLES FOR
150  REM                      PRINT USING STATEMENTS
160  REM
170  REM ************************************
180  TOTAL = 0
190  A$ = "\                  \        ###        $##,###.##"
200  B$ = "SUM OF AMOUNTS                         $##,###.##"
210  PRINT "NAME               HOURS      AMT EARNED"
220  FOR I=1 TO 3
230     READ EMPLOYEE$,RATE,HOURS
240     AMOUNT = RATE * HOURS
250     TOTAL = TOTAL + AMOUNT
260     PRINT USING A$;EMPLOYEE$,HOURS,AMOUNT
270  NEXT I
280  PRINT USING B$;TOTAL
290  DATA "JONES",6.5,160
300  DATA "SMITH",12.16,200
310  DATA "BAKER",5,100
320  END

RUN
NAME               HOURS      AMT EARNED
JONES               160       $ 1,040.00
SMITH               200       $ 2,432.00
BAKER               100       $   500.00
SUM OF AMOUNTS                $ 3,972.00
```

<code>#,###.##</code>

specifies that 1245.06 be printed as

<code>1,245.06</code>

If a number to be output with the last image is smaller than 1,000, the comma is replaced by a ƀ. Thus, 154.68 is output as

<code>ƀƀ154.68</code>

You should note that the # is a special symbol when used to specify an output image.

String Variables.   The symbol pair \ \ is used to specify the maximum number of characters printed out for a string variable. The backslashes plus each space left between them represent the length of output. For example, a declaration such as

$$\backslash \not{b}\not{b}\not{b} \backslash$$

will accommodate the full contents of any output strings of five characters or fewer.

Constants.   Generally any characters other than # (for numeric variables) and the backslashes (for string variables) will be printed as they appear. Thus, the dollar sign in lines 190 and 200 and the phrase SUM OF AMOUNTS in line 200 appear on the output exactly as they do in the output image.

As you can see by inspecting the program in Figure 4-2, a major advantage of PRINT USING is that it allows neat decimal-point alignment in columns. This is a must for reports used in business. The use of comma spacing or the TAB function does not provide this luxury, since variable values start printing in the zone boundary or tab stop indicated, leaving the decimal point to fall where it may. This can be seen in Figure 4-1; note that the gross pay for Ann Jones is not neatly lined up under the gross pay of the other individuals.

The values of string variables automatically begin at the far left (left-justified) within the \ \ symbol pair. The values of numeric variables are aligned with respect to the decimal point. The following example should make this clear:

```
10  N$="BETSY JONES "
20  A=10
30  B=3.06
40  A$="\               \    ###    ###.##"
50  PRINT USING A$;N$,A,B
60  END
RUN
BETSY JONES        10     3.06
```

First # field   Second #   Third # field
(15 characters)   field   (3 characters
                     (3 characters) to left of decimal point,
                                     2 characters to right)

If the values of any of the variables are too large to fit within the specified \ \ or #-sign fields, either truncation, rounding, or output suppression (that is, spaces or nonnumeric symbols) may occur. Referring to the last example, if

```
N$="SHERIDAN P. WHITESIDE"
A=10.6
B=8321.46
```

the following output might be produced:

```
SHERIDAN P.  WHIbbbbb11bbb******
```
        Truncation   Rounding Output
                                         suppression

Solved Review Problems

Example 1

Compute the square root ($I^{1/2}$), cube root ($I^{1/3}$), and fourth root ($I^{1/4}$) of all integers I in the range 1–10. The output should be neatly labeled and formatted.

Solution

The program and associated output are shown in Figure 4-3. You should note the use of the comma in lines 210 and 250, which keeps the output device printing on the same line. The blank PRINT statement in line 270 is extremely important; it negates the effect of the comma on line 250 when the fourth roots are printed and sends the output device to the next output line.

Example 2

Straight-line depreciation expenses are computed by the formula:

$$\text{Annual depreciation charge} = \frac{\text{Original cost} - \text{Salvage value}}{\text{Useful life}}$$

Provide a depreciation schedule for a car that originally cost $7,328 and will be worth approximately $600 at the end of its 10-year useful life. The depreciation schedule should show (for each year) the depreciation charge, total depreciation so far, and the (undepreciated) balance.

Solution

The program and associated output are shown in Figure 4-4.

The annual depreciation charge is computed in line 260. Because the charge for each year is the same, it is computed before the FOR/NEXT loop beginning in line 300. This loop is used to compute the total accumulated depreciation, compute the undepreciated balance, and produce most of the output lines for the report. The PRINT USING statement in line 330 aligns the output neatly in formatted columns.

Example 3

The TAB function is extremely helpful for printing various types of geometric designs. The program in Figure 4-5 uses the TAB function to print a triangle.

The triangle in the figure consists of 11 lines of output. The top line of 21 asterisks and the bottom line of 1 asterisk are each produced by a single statement—statements 170 and 270, respectively. The nine middle lines of output consist of two asterisks each and are produced in the FOR/NEXT loop, using the variables LEFT and RIGHT. As each pass is made in the loop, LEFT (which is initialized to 1) increases by one unit and RIGHT (which is initialized to 21) decreases by one unit, producing the collapsing sides of the triangle.

Figure 4-3   A program for computing roots.

```
10  REM     TITLE: PROGRAM 4-3
20  REM
30  REM     DESCRIPTION: THIS PROGRAM COMPUTES THE
40  REM       SQUARE ROOT, CUBE ROOT, AND FOURTH ROOT
50  REM       OF ALL INTEGERS IN THE RANGE 1-10
60  REM
70  REM     AUTHOR: C.S. PARKER
80  REM     DATE: 10/5/91
90  REM
100 REM     I       = LOOP VARIABLE TO GENERATE 1-10
110 REM     N       = LOOP VARIABLE TO GENERATE EXPONENTS
120 REM     ROOT    = THE COMPUTED ROOT
130 REM
140 REM ********************************************
150 PRINT TAB(20);"COMPUTATIONS TABLE"
160 PRINT
170 PRINT "INTEGER","SQUARE ROOT","CUBE ROOT","FOURTH ROOT"
180 PRINT
190 FOR I = 1 TO 10
200    REM PRINT OUT ROW NUMBER
210    PRINT I,
220    FOR N = 0 TO 4
230       REM COMPUTE AND PRINT OUT THE REST OF THE ROW
240       ROOT = I ^ (1/N)
250       PRINT ROOT,
260    NEXT N
270    PRINT
280 NEXT I
290 END

RUN
                    COMPUTATIONS TABLE
```

INTEGER	SQUARE ROOT	CUBE ROOT	FOURTH ROOT
1	1	1	1
2	1.414213	1.259921	1.189207
3	1.732051	1.44225	1.316074
4	2	1.587401	1.414214
5	2.236068	1.709976	1.495349
6	2.44949	1.817121	1.565085
7	2.645751	1.912931	1.626577
8	2.828427	2	1.681793
9	3	2.080084	1.732051
10	3.162278	2.154435	1.778279

Figure 4-4   A depreciation problem.

```
10   REM     TITLE: PROGRAM 4-4
20   REM
30   REM     DESCRIPTION: THIS PROGRAM COMPUTES STRAIGHT-LINE
40   REM     DEPRECIATION CHARGES FOR AN AUTOMOBILE
50   REM
60   REM     AUTHOR: C.S. PARKER
70   REM     DATE: 10/5/91
80   REM
90   REM     COST      = ORIGINAL COST OF AUTO
100  REM     LIFE      = USEFUL LIFE
110  REM     SALVAGE   = SALVAGE VALUE AT END OF USEFUL LIFE
120  REM     ANNUAL    = ANNUAL DEPRECIATION CHARGE
130  REM     ACCUM     = ACCUMULATED DEPRECIATION
140  REM     UNDEP     = UNDEPRECIATED BALANCE
150  REM     I         = LOOP VARIABLE
160  REM     A$        = OUTPUT-IMAGE VARIABLE
170  REM
180  REM ***************************************************
190  A$=" ##       $#,###.##         $#,###.##        $#,###.##"
200  PRINT TAB(12);"AUTO DEPRECIATION SCHEDULE"
210  PRINT
220  PRINT "YEAR    DEPR CHARGE        ACCUM DEP       UNDEP BALANCE"
230  PRINT
240  READ COST,SALVAGE,LIFE
250  REM DEPRECIATION CALCULATION
260  ANNUAL = (COST - SALVAGE) / LIFE
270  ACCUM = 0
280  UNDEP = COST
290  REM PERFORM OTHER CALCULATIONS AND OUTPUT RESULTS
300  FOR I = 1 TO LIFE
310     ACCUM = ACCUM + ANNUAL
320     UNDEP = UNDEP - ANNUAL
330     PRINT USING A$;I,ANNUAL, ACCUM, UNDEP
340  NEXT I
350  DATA 7328,600,10
360  END

RUN
             AUTO DEPRECIATION SCHEDULE

   YEAR    DEPR CHARGE        ACCUM DEP       UNDEP BALANCE

     1     $   672.80        $   672.80       $6,655.20
     2     $   672.80        $1,345.60        $5,982.40
     3     $   672.80        $2,018.40        $5,309.60
     4     $   672.80        $2,691.20        $4,636.80
     5     $   672.80        $3,364.00        $3,964.00
     6     $   672.80        $4,036.80        $3,291.20
     7     $   672.80        $4,709.60        $2,618.40
     8     $   672.80        $5,382.40        $1,945.60
     9     $   672.80        $6,055.20        $1,272.80
    10     $   672.80        $6,728.00        $   600.00
```

Figure 4-5   A program, flowchart, and pseudocode for producing a triangle.

Program

```
10   REM    TITLE: PROGRAM 4-5
20   REM
30   REM    DESCRIPTION: THIS PROGRAM MAKES A TRIANGLE
40   REM
50   REM    AUTHOR: C.S. PARKER
60   REM    DATE: 10/5/91
70   REM
80   REM    LEFT  = POSITION OF LEFTMOST ASTERISK
90   REM    RIGHT = POSITION OF RIGHTMOST ASTERISK
100  REM    I     = LOOP VARIABLE
110  REM
120  REM ****************************************
130  LEFT = 1
140  RIGHT = 21
150  REM
160  REM FIRST, PRINT THE TOP LINE OF ASTERISKS
170  PRINT "*********************"
180  REM
190  REM SECOND, PRINT THE MIDDLE LINES
200  FOR I = 1 TO 9
210     LEFT = LEFT + 1
220     RIGHT = RIGHT - 1
230     PRINT TAB(LEFT);"*";TAB(RIGHT);"*"
240  NEXT I
250  REM
260  REM THIRD, PRINT THE BOTTOMMOST ASTERISK
270  PRINT TAB(11);"*"
280  END
```

```
                    RUN
        *********************
          *                 *
           *               *
            *             *
             *           *
              *         *
               *       *
                *     *
                 *   *
                  * *
                   *
```

Flowchart

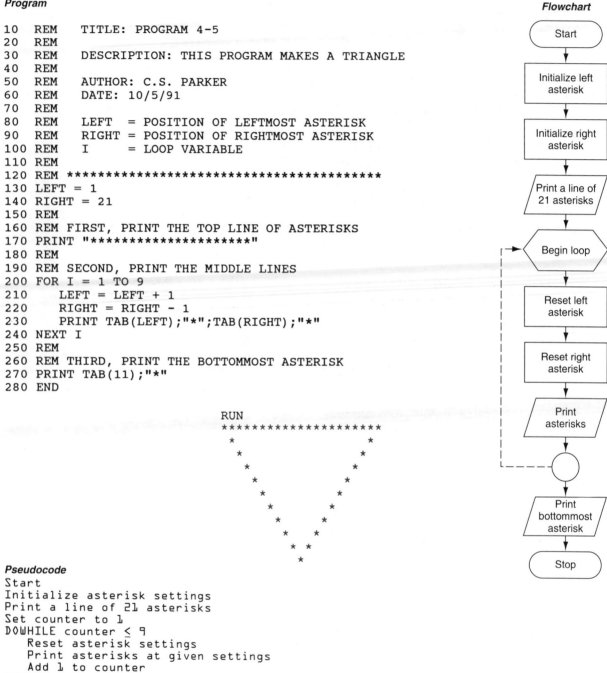

Pseudocode

```
Start
Initialize asterisk settings
Print a line of 21 asterisks
Set counter to 1
DOWHILE counter ≤ 9
   Reset asterisk settings
   Print asterisks at given settings
   Add 1 to counter
END DO
Print bottommost asterisk
Stop
```

Example 4

The following table lists salespeople at XYZ Company, their branch affiliations, and the amount of their sales booked last week:

Name	Branch	Sales
M. Vincent	A	$1,020
T. Loux	A	$1,090
J. Jefferson	A	$1,400
A. T. Jones	A	$1,700
C. Smith	B	$1,100
L. Martinez	B	$1,400
M. Schurer	C	$1,550
G. Seaver	C	$1,090

Write a program that outputs salespeople (and their sales) by branch, subtotals sales by branch, and calculates a grand total over all branches.

Solution

The program and associated output are shown in Figure 4-6. The subtotals that "foot" each branch are examples of *control breaks*. In the program, variable BRANCH$ (branch) is referred to as the *control-break variable*. BRANCH$ "breaks" two times—when branch changes from A to B and later from B to C. At each break, a subtotal is printed. Before the program ends, it prints out the final subtotal and the grand total. The program uses a "holding variable" (HOLD$) to hold the value of BRANCH$ from the most recently processed record and uses a check (in line 260) to signal when a new record represents a change in branch. For this program to work, the data must be presorted by branch.

Exercises

Instructions: Provide an answer to each of the following questions.

1. Consider this program:

```
10 FOR I=1 TO 3
20 PRINT "HELLO NUMBER";I
30 FOR J=1 TO 4
40 PRINT X=I*J,
50 NEXT J
60 PRINT
70 NEXT I
```

   a. How many lines will be printed by this program?
   b. How many times will line 20 be executed?
   c. What will be the fourth line printed by this program?
   d. How many times will line 40 be executed?
   e. What will be the value of X at the end of the program?

2. How would your answers to Exercise 1 change if the following changes were made to the program?

Figure 4-6   A control-break program and output (inset).

```
10  REM     TITLE: PROGRAM 4-6
20  REM
30  REM     DESCRIPTION: THIS PROGRAM COMPUTES BRANCH
40  REM        SUBTOTALS AND THE GRAND TOTAL
50  REM
60  REM     AUTHOR: C.S. PARKER
70  REM     DATE: 10/5/90
80  REM
90  REM     SUBTOTAL  = BRANCH SUBTOTAL
100 REM     GRAND     = GRAND TOTAL
110 REM     PERSON$   = SALESPERSON NAME
120 REM     SALES     = SALESPERSON SALES
130 REM     BRANCH$   = BRANCH
140 REM     HOLD$     = HOLDING VARIABLE FOR BRANCH
150 REM
160 REM ****************************************
170 SUBTOTAL = 0
180 GRAND = 0
190 PRINT TAB(10);"XYZ SALES REPORT"
200 PRINT
210 PRINT "NAME","SALES"
220 PRINT
230 READ PERSON$,BRANCH$,SALES
240 HOLD$ = BRANCH$
250 WHILE PERSON$ <> "LAST RECORD"
260    IF BRANCH$ = HOLD$ THEN 320
270       PRINT
280       PRINT "   SUBTOTAL - BRANCH ";HOLD$,SUBTOTAL
290       PRINT
300       SUBTOTAL = 0
310       HOLD$ = BRANCH$
320    GRAND = GRAND + SALES
330    SUBTOTAL = SUBTOTAL + SALES
340    PRINT PERSON$,SALES
350    READ PERSON$,BRANCH$,SALES
360 WEND
370 PRINT
380 PRINT "   SUBTOTAL - BRANCH ";HOLD$,SUBTOTAL
390 PRINT
400 PRINT "   GRAND TOTAL",GRAND
410 REM *********DATA STATEMENTS***************
420 DATA "M. VINCENT","A",1020,"T. LOUX","A",1090
430 DATA "J. JEFFERSON","A",1400,"A.T. JONES","A",1700
440 DATA "C. SMITH","B",1100,"L. MARTINEZ","B",1400
450 DATA "M. SCHURER","C",1550,"G. SEAVER","C",1090
460 DATA "LAST RECORD","Z",0
470 REM ****************************************
480 END
```

```
          XYZ SALES REPORT

NAME               SALES

M. VINCENT         1020
T. LOUX            1090
J. JEFFERSON       1400
A.T. JONES         1700

   SUBTOTAL - BRANCH A   5210

C. SMITH           1100
L. MARTINEZ        1400

   SUBTOTAL - BRANCH B   2500

M. SCHURER         1550
G. SEAVER          1090

   SUBTOTAL - BRANCH C   2640

   GRAND TOTAL             10350
```

```
 5 LET X=0
35 LET X=X+I*J
40 PRINT X,
```

3. Consider the following program:

```
10 READ A,B,C,D,E
20 PRINT...
30 DATA (data values)
```

Write a PRINT statement for line 20 that will do the following:
a. Place the values of A, B, and C in print zones 1, 2, and 3, respectively.
b. Place the value of A in all five print zones.
c. Place the values of C, D, and E in print zones 3, 4, and 5, respectively.
d. Place the values of A, B, and C in print zones 1, 3, and 5, respectively.

4. Assume X has a value of 2590.86. Show how this value would be output when assigned to the output-image fields below. (Use Ƀ to represent a blank space.)

a. `####`   c. `$#,###`
b. `##,###.##`   d. `#.##`

5. Assume N$ has a value of JONES. Show how this value would be output when assigned to the output-image fields below. (Use Ƀ to represent a blank space.)

a. `\ƀƀƀƀƀƀ\`   c. `\ƀ\`
b. `\ƀƀƀ\`   d. `#####`

Programming Problems

Instructions: Write a BASIC program to do each of the following tasks.

1. Students in a class are required to take three exams. The class performed as follows on the exams last semester:

Student Name	Scores		
	Exam 1	Exam 2	Exam 3
Jo Smith	70	80	90
Ed Lynn	40	65	59
Richard Johnson	86	93	72
Linda Harris	95	75	86
Wendy Williams	77	83	78
David Rudolph	55	83	78

Compute the average on each of the 3 exams, the average of each of the 6 students, and the overall average of the 18 scores. Print the table with these computed averages shown in their appropriate row and column positions. Use trailer values at the end of your data list so that your program can sense when there are no more records to be read.

2. Solve Problem 1 by printing letter grades in place of the average score of each of the six students. Use the following formula to assign grades to numbers: 90 and above = A, 80–89 = B, 70–79 = C, 60–69 = D, below 60 = F.

3. Redo the following table so that all of the decimal points line up and each column of data is centered below its column title:

```
NAME             GROSS PAY
----             ---------

ZELDA SMITH   $ 1000
ZEB TSOSIE    $ 83.25
ZENON JONES   $ .50
```

4. If *P* dollars are invested in an account today at a compounded interest rate of *R* percent per period, the amount in the account at the end of *N* periods is given by

$$S = P(1 + R/100)^N$$

For example, $100 will be worth $129.15 on 12/31/94 if it was invested on 12/31/89 at an interest rate of 5.25 percent compounded annually; that is,

$$S = 100 \, (1 + 5.25/100)^5$$
$$= 100 \, (1.0525)^5 = 129.15$$

Produce a table showing the value of $1 at the end of 1, 2, 3, . . ., 10 years at interest rates of 10 percent, 10.5 percent, 11 percent, 11.5 percent, and 12 percent. The years should appear as rows of the table and the interest rates as columns. Make sure that your decimal points are lined up so that your output looks neat and professional.

5. Figure 4-5 shows how to use the TAB function to produce a triangle. Use the TAB function to produce a square with 10 asterisks on each side.

6. The program given in Figure 4-5 shows how to produce a hollow triangle. Revise this program so that the triangle is completely filled with asterisks.

7. Redo the program in Figure 4-4 using the sum-of-the-year's digits depreciation method, which works as the following example shows: Assume that an asset originally costs $4000, has a salvage value of $1000, and has a useful life of 3 years. The asset will be depreciated by $3000 ($4000 minus $1000) over the 3-year period. The sum of the year's digits for 3 years is 1 + 2 + 3 = 6. The procedure to compute the depreciation charge for each of the 3 years is given below:

$$\text{Year 1: } (3/6) * \$3000 = \$1500$$
$$\text{Year 2: } (2/6) * \$3000 = \$1000$$
$$\text{Year 3: } (1/6) * \$3000 = \underline{\$\ 500}$$
$$\$3000$$

Note, in the computations above, that the fraction's denominator is always the sum of the year's digits. This is computed by the formula $n(n + 1)/2$, where *n* is the asset's useful life. The fraction's numerator is, for year *i*, equal to $n - i + 1$. The fraction is always multiplied by a constant amount, which is equal to the cost minus the salvage value.

SECTION 5
ADVANCED TOPICS

Subscripting

Subscripting is one of the most useful tools in BASIC, enabling the programmer to build and store lists of numbers or strings. Such lists are commonly called *arrays*. A subscript is simply a number that refers to a position in the list or array. For example, suppose we wanted to place the data in the "averages" program of Figure 3-1 (page 44) in a list. If we decided to call the list X, it might look as follows:

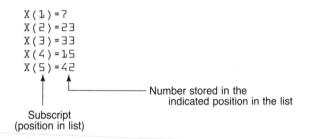

$$X(1) = 7$$
$$X(2) = 23$$
$$X(3) = 33$$
$$X(4) = 15$$
$$X(5) = 42$$

Number stored in the
indicated position in the list

Subscript
(position in list)

You should make certain that you fully grasp the difference between a position in the list and the number stored in that position before reading further. If, for example, you were asked if $X(3) < X(4)$, how would you respond? (*Note:* 33 is not less than 15, so the answer is no.)

A Simple Subscripting Problem

Let's again find the average of a set of numbers, expanding the problem to 12 values. Also, let's assume that we wish to output the difference of each of the numbers in the list from the average. A program for solving this problem is shown in Figure 5-1. As usual, study the problem carefully before reading the commentary that follows.

The first thing you may have noticed in Figure 5-1 is the DIM (dimension) statement in line 170. This statement instructs the computer to reserve 12* storage positions for array NUMBER. This is necessary because each number in the array is assigned to a different variable—that is, NUMBER(1), NUMBER(2), . . ., NUMBER(12)—and, as is the usual practice, each variable corresponds to a single

---

*Many versions of BASIC will also reserve a 13th storage location, for NUMBER(0). Many skilled programmers, however, choose to ignore this storage position, because other programming languages often prohibit a zero subscript.

Figure 5-1
A program for computing differences of numbers in a list from the average of the list.

```
10   REM     TITLE: PROGRAM 5-1
20   REM
30   REM     DESCRIPTION: THIS PROGRAM COMPUTES THE DIFFERENCES
40   REM        BETWEEN NUMBERS IN A LIST AND THE LIST AVERAGE
50   REM
60   REM     AUTHOR: C.S. PARKER
70   REM     DATE: 10/5/91
80   REM
90   REM     I       = THE LOOP VARIABLE
100  REM     NUMBER  = A NUMBER IN THE LIST
110  REM     LENGTH  = THE NUMBER OF NUMBERS IN THE LIST
120  REM     SUM     = THE SUM OF THE NUMBERS IN THE LIST
130  REM     AVERAGE = THE AVERAGE OF THE NUMBERS
140  REM     DEV     = THE DEVIATION OF A NUMBER FROM AVERAGE
150  REM
160  REM ****************************************************
170  DIM NUMBER(12)
180  LET SUM = 0
190  READ LENGTH
200  REM
210  REM READ AND SUM NUMBERS
220  FOR I = 1 TO LENGTH
230      READ NUMBER(I)
240      LET SUM = SUM + NUMBER(I)
250  NEXT I
260  LET AVERAGE = SUM / LENGTH
270  PRINT "NUMBER","AVERAGE","DIFFERENCE"
280  PRINT
290  REM
300  REM RECALL VALUES, COMPUTE DEVIATIONS, AND OUTPUT RESULTS
310  FOR I = 1 TO LENGTH
320      LET DEV = NUMBER(I) - AVERAGE
330      PRINT NUMBER(I),AVERAGE,DEV
340  NEXT I
350  DATA 12
360  DATA 5,10,11,13,4,6,8,14,2,15,1,7
370  END

RUN
NUMBER          AVERAGE         DIFFERENCE
  5               8               -3
 10               8                2
 11               8                3
 13               8                5
  4               8               -4
  6               8               -2
  8               8                0
 14               8                6
  2               8               -6
 15               8                7
  1               8               -7
  7               8               -1
```

storage location. Thus, a total of 17 storage positions will be allocated to the variables in this program, as follows:

```
NUMBER(1), NUMBER(2), NUMBER(3), . . ., NUMBER(12)
```

Specified by the DIM
statement

```
SUM, LENGTH, I, AVERAGE, DEV
```

Nonsubscripted
variables
in program

Many versions of BASIC will allow you to omit the DIM statement if the length of the array stored is 10 positions or fewer. In other words, if there were 10 or fewer numbers in line 360, the computer would react as if you had specified

```
170 DIM NUMBER(10)
```

in your program if this statement is absent. This is called *implicit* dimensioning. Most skilled programmers, however, prefer *explicit* dimensioning, in which all arrays are declared in one or more DIM statements. The reasons for this are similar to the ones for explicitly initializing count and sum variables to zero: The intent is made clear, the opportunity for mistakes is minimized, and the practice is a good one to adopt if you program in other languages (BASIC is among a minority of languages permitting implicit dimensioning).

Since the array in our program has 12 positions, NUMBER must be dimensioned explicitly. If the DIM statement is absent, the computer will not automatically reserve space for NUMBER(11) and NUMBER(12). Thus, the program will "bomb" when the computer attempts to manipulate one of these variables. It is acceptable, however, to reserve more storage positions in a DIM statement than you will actually use.

The DIM statement, like the DATA statement, is not executed by the computer. Although there are several acceptable places to position it, it is good practice to put it at the beginning of the program to avoid potential problems.

If several arrays need to be dimensioned, it is possible to use one DIM statement or several. For example, both

```
10 DIM A(250),X(15),Y(20),Z(200),T(6)
```

and the combination

```
10 DIM A(250),X(15)
20 DIM Y(20),Z(200),T(6)
```

are acceptable to dimension the five arrays shown.

Another interesting feature of the program in Figure 5-1 concerns statements 230 and 240, which are contained in the first loop. Each time I is incremented, a single number is taken from statement 360 and assigned to the Ith variable in the NUMBER array. Thus, when I = 1, NUMBER(1) is assigned 5; when I = 2,

NUMBER(2) is assigned 10; and so on. When the computer exits the first loop and makes the computation in line 260, storage looks as follows:*

NUMBER(1) 5	NUMBER(2) 10	NUMBER(3) 11	NUMBER(4) 13
NUMBER(5) 4	NUMBER(6) 6	NUMBER(7) 8	NUMBER(8) 14
NUMBER(9) 2	NUMBER(10) 15	NUMBER(11) 1	NUMBER(12) 7
SUM 96	I 12	LENGTH 12	AVERAGE 8
DEV 0			

When the second loop is encountered (line 310), the computer has all the information it needs in storage to compute the 12 differences (DEV = NUMBER(I) − AVERAGE). Thus, all that needs to be done in this loop is to successively recall from storage NUMBER(1), NUMBER(2), . . ., NUMBER(12), subtract AVERAGE from each of these values, and compute the differences, DEV.

You should note that it would be extremely inconvenient to solve a problem like the one in Figure 5-1 without the use of subscripts. This is because we need to consider the values in the array twice—once to compute the average and again to compute the differences.

The general format of the DIM statement is as follows:

> Line # DIM list of arrays (separated by commas)

String Lists

The example provided in the previous subsections illustrated a list of *numbers*. BASIC also allows the programmer to form lists of *strings*. For example, suppose we wish to create a list of fruits (say, APPLES, ORANGES, BANANAS, PEACHES, and CHERRIES) and then output the list in reverse order. The program in Figure 5-2 does just this. Note that subscripted string variables are named in the same way as unsubscripted *(scalar)* ones—a string of characters followed by the dollar sign.

Double Subscripting

Data to be processed by the computer system are sometimes better represented in two-dimensional (table) form than in one-dimensional (list) form. For example, consider the following data, which show the vote distribution on a certain issue in different schools of a university:

	Voted Yes	Voted No	Didn't Vote
Business	205	152	38
Liberal arts	670	381	115
Engineering	306	251	47
Forestry	112	33	14

*In some versions of BASIC, I would be set to 13 even though the loop was executed only 12 times. This is because the first time NEXT is encountered, I is set to 2; the twelfth and last time NEXT is encountered, I is set to 13. Some computer systems will "roll back" this value to 12 upon leaving the loop.

```
10  REM    TITLE: PROGRAM 5-2
20  REM
30  REM    DESCRIPTION:  THIS PROGRAM ILLUSTRATES HOW TO
40  REM       HANDLE STRING DATA IN AN ARRAY
50  REM
60  REM    AUTHOR: C.S. PARKER
70  REM    DATE: 10/5/91
80  REM
90  REM    I      = LOOP VARIABLE
100 REM    FRUIT$ = AN ARRAY STORING THE NAME OF FRUITS
110 REM
120 REM ********************************************
130 DIM FRUIT$(5)
140 REM
150 REM READ A LIST OF FRUITS
160 FOR I = 1 TO 5
170     READ FRUIT$(I)
180 NEXT I
190 REM
200 REM PRINT OUT THE LIST IN REVERSE ORDER
210 FOR I = 5 TO 1 STEP -1
220     PRINT FRUIT$(I)
230 NEXT I
240 DATA "APPLES","ORANGES","BANANAS"
250 DATA "PEACHES","CHERRIES"
260 END

RUN
CHERRIES
PEACHES
BANANAS
ORANGES
APPLES
```

Figure 5-2
A program that manipulates a string list.

These data, which include four rows and three columns of numbers, exist naturally in the form of a table. It would be most convenient if we could give the table a name (ARRAY, for example) and store any number in the table with reference to its row and column position. For example, 115, which is in row 2 and column 3, would be referenced by the subscripted variable ARRAY(2, 3).

Fortunately, BASIC permits us to represent two-dimensional tables in the simple manner just described. Thus, we could store the table numbers in the following 12 variables:

ARRAY(1, 1) = 205	ARRAY(1, 2) = 152	ARRAY(1, 3) = 38
ARRAY(2, 1) = 670	ARRAY(2, 2) = 381	ARRAY(2, 3) = 115
ARRAY(3, 1) = 306	ARRAY(3, 2) = 251	ARRAY(3, 3) = 47
ARRAY(4, 1) = 112	ARRAY(4, 2) = 33	ARRAY(4, 3) = 14

It is relatively easy to create such a table in BASIC and to later access each number and process it as needed. To see how this might be done, refer to the program in Figure 5-3, which totals all of the numbers in the table and subsequently divides each number in the table by this total.

You should observe that in this program, as is the usual practice with subscripts, a DIM statement is immediately employed to declare the size of the table. Then nested loops are established in statements 200–250 to automatically generate

Figure 5-3
A program that reads a table, totals all the numbers in the table, and prints the fraction that each number is with regard to the sum.

```
10   REM    TITLE: PROGRAM 5-3
20   REM
30   REM    DESCRIPTION:  THIS PROGRAM OUTPUTS AN ARRAY OF
40   REM       NUMBERS, TOTALS IT, AND OUTPUTS EACH ARRAY
50   REM       VALUE AS A FRACTION OF THE TOTAL
60   REM
70   REM    AUTHOR: C.S. PARKER
80   REM    DATE: 10/5/91
90   REM
100  REM    ARRAY    = THE ARRAY OF NUMBERS
110  REM    I,J,M,N  = LOOP VARIABLES
120  REM    SUM      = THE SUM OF ALL NUMBERS IN THE ARRAY
130  REM    FRACTION = THE FRACTION OBTAINED
140  REM
150  REM    **************************************************
160  DIM ARRAY(4,3)
170  SUM = 0
180  REM
190  REM READ NUMBERS INTO ARRAY AND TOTAL THEM
200  FOR I = 1 TO 4
210     FOR J = 1 TO 3
220         READ ARRAY(I,J)
230         SUM = SUM + ARRAY(I,J)
240     NEXT J
250  NEXT I
260  REM
270  REM COMPUTE FRACTIONS AND OUTPUT RESULTS
280  FOR M = 1 TO 4
290     FOR N = 1 TO 3
300         FRACTION = ARRAY(M,N) / SUM
310         PRINT FRACTION,
320     NEXT N
330     PRINT
340  NEXT M
350  DATA 205,152,38
360  DATA 670,381,115
370  DATA 306,251,47
380  DATA 112,33,14
390  END

RUN
 .088210        .065405        .016351
 .288296        .163941        .049484
 .131670        .108003        .020224
 .048193        .014200        .006024
```

the row (I = 1, 2, 3, 4) and column (J = 1, 2, 3) subscripts. Thus, the first time these nested loops are executed,

I = 1, J = 1, ARRAY(1, 1) is assigned 205, and SUM = 0 + 205 = 205

The second time,

I = 1, J = 2, ARRAY(1, 2) is assigned 152, and SUM = 205 + 152 = 357

and so forth.

In the nested loops in statements 280–330, we simply recall ARRAY(1, 1), ARRAY(1, 2), . . ., ARRAY(4, 3) successively from storage and, as we do so, divide each by the table sum and print out the fraction obtained. Note that the variables (M, N) used to represent the subscripts in the second set of nested loops are different than those (I, J) used in the first set. Although we could have used I and J again, the example illustrates that any choice of a subscript variable will do as long as the proper numbers are substituted by the computer to represent the row and column involved.

Two final points on the program in Figure 5-3 deserve your close attention. First, note that the PRINT statement in line 310 contains a comma. This keeps output belonging in the same row printing on the same line. Second, note the blank PRINT statement on line 330. This statement forces the output device onto a new line, where a new row of numbers is printed.

Functions

A *function* is a precoded formula that is referenced in a computer program. BASIC permits two types of functions: *library (built-in) functions* and *user-defined functions*. Two widely used library functions are INT and RND, which truncate and generate random numbers, respectively. Since these functions are built into the BASIC language, the computer system knows exactly what type of action to take when it runs into one of them. Many other library functions are probably available with the version of BASIC used by your computer system. Following is a partial list of some of the more common ones:

Function	Purpose
ABS(X)	Returns the absolute value of X
SQR(X)	Calculates the square root of X (X must be $>=0$)
RND	Returns a random number between .000000 and .999999
SIN(X)	Computes the sine of X (X must be in radians)
COS(X)	Computes the cosine of X (X must be in radians)
TAN(X)	Computes the tangent of X (X must be in radians)
LOG(X)	Calculates the natural logarithm of X (X must be positive)
EXP(X)	Calculates the term e^x, where e is approximately 2.718
INT(X)	Returns the greatest integer $<=X$

You can also define your own functions. This can be useful when there is a formula you need to use repeatedly that is not a library function. User-defined functions are specified with the DEF statement. For example, suppose we wanted to compute the commission earned by a salesperson as

☐   15 percent of gross sales of brand-name items

☐   10 percent of gross sales of nonbrand items

Thus, if DUMM1 represents gross sales of brand-name items and DUMM2 is gross sales of nonbrand items, the commission, C, may be calculated as

```
C=.15*DUMM1+.10*DUMM2
```

A program that computes this commission for three salespeople is given in Figure 5-4. You should inspect this program carefully before proceeding further.

Figure 5-4 Use of a user-defined function to compute commissions.

```
10   REM    TITLE: PROGRAM 5-4
20   REM
30   REM    DESCRIPTION:  THIS PROGRAM COMPUTES SALES
40   REM       COMMISSIONS USING FUNCTIONS
50   REM
60   REM    AUTHOR: C.S. PARKER
70   REM    DATE: 10/5/91
80   REM
90   REM    I            = LOOP VARIABLE
100  REM    DUMM1,DUMM2 = DUMMY ARGUMENTS
110  REM    REAL1,REAL2 = REAL ARGUMENTS
120  REM    PERSON$      = SALESPERSON NAME
130  REM
140  REM    ************************************************
150  DEF FNC(DUMM1,DUMM2) = .15 * DUMM1 + .1 * DUMM2   ◄── The function is defined here
160  FOR I = 1 TO 3
170     READ PERSON$,REAL1,REAL2
180     PRINT PERSON$,FNC(REAL1,REAL2)   ◄── The function is executed here
190  NEXT I
200  DATA "JOE SMITH",700.00,1000.00
210  DATA "ZELDA GREY",600.00,1200.00
220  DATA "SUE JOHNSON",1000.00,500.00
230  END

RUN
JOE SMITH        205
ZELDA GREY       210
SUE JOHNSON      200
```

Note in the program that the formula for computing the commissions is defined in line 150. The formula must be defined (with a DEF statement) before it can be used (as in statement 180).

The format of the DEF statement is

$$\text{Line \# DEF FNx (y) = z}$$

where x is a single alphabetic letter or string of letters chosen by the programmer, y is a list of arguments, and z is a valid BASIC expression. It is also permissible to use several DEF statements in a single program. Note that the word DEF must be followed by a space and then FN. You must remember, however, to define the functions early in your program, *before* you reference them.

You should also note that the formula, or function, in the figure also contains two *dummy arguments*, arbitrarily named DUMM1 and DUMM2. The only significance of dummy arguments is that they demonstrate how the function will be computed. After reading in the salesperson information in line 170, the computer system prints out in line 180 the salesperson's name and total commission due. Before the computer calculates and prints the commission, it "refers" to line 150 and substitutes REAL1 for DUMM1 and REAL2 for DUMM2.

REAL1 and REAL2, also arbitrarily named, are called *real arguments*. Real arguments are always substituted for corresponding dummy arguments, according to their respective positioning within the parentheses, whenever the function is used in the program. The program could also have been written by using the same variable names as both dummy and real arguments.

This ability to define a function is one of the most useful and most powerful features of BASIC. It is also the capability most overlooked, even by many skilled programmers.

File Processing

Most business applications in real life involve the processing of enormous amounts of data. Typically, when such applications are coded in a language like BASIC, these data are stored in independent files, apart from the programs that use them. There are several reasons why this practice is followed. Three of the most important ones are the following:

☐ **Processing Feasibility.** Primary memory is often not large enough to store a complete set of data at one time. Consequently, it is easier to manage data independently from programs, bringing only specific pieces of data into primary memory on an "as needed" basis.

☐ **Less Storage.** Most data serve multiple purposes; that is, they are used by more than one program. For example, data on customer purchases and payments can be used by both a program that prepares customer billings and by a program that determines which customers are delinquent in their payment (and must be sent a reminder). So, when data are stored separately from programs, several programs can access the same body of data, requiring less storage space.

☐ **Better Data Integrity.** When data are physically independent of their programs, the *integrity* of the data is higher. This means that when a change is made in any body of data, the change is reflected consistently in all of the applications that use it.

Versions of BASIC can differ substantially with respect to the way in which they process files. Here, to keep matters simple, we will cover only the convention that works on IBM microcomputers and compatible machines and also will cover only one type of file—*sequential files.*

Organizing Data into Files. When putting data into files, it is customary to first organize the data into fields and records. The terms "field," "record," and "file" each have a precise meaning in a computing environment, and you should use them with care.

A *field* is a collection of characters (a character is a single digit, letter of the alphabet, or special symbol such as the decimal point) that represents a single type of data. A *record* is a collection of related fields, and a *file* is a collection of related records. Files, with their associated records and fields, are normally stored on input/output media such as disks and tapes.

A college, for example, probably would have a file on disk of all students currently enrolled. This file would contain a record for each student. Each record would have several fields—one each for the student's ID number, name, street, city, state, local address, local phone number, major subject area, and so on.

Figure 5-5
A program that creates a sequential file.

```
10  REM      TITLE:   PROGRAM 5-5
20  REM
30  REM      DESCRIPTION: THIS PROGRAM CREATES A
40  REM         SEQUENTIAL FILE
50  REM
60  REM      AUTHOR: C.S. PARKER
70  REM      DATE: 10/5/91
80  REM
90  REM      EMPLOYEE$   = EMPLOYEE NAME
100 REM      RATE        = PAY RATE
110 REM      GROSS       = GROSS PAY
120 REM
130 REM ****************************************
140 OPEN "B:PAYFILE" FOR OUTPUT AS #1
150 READ EMPLOYEE$,RATE,GROSS
160 WHILE EMPLOYEE$ <> "LAST RECORD"
170     WRITE #1,EMPLOYEE$,RATE,GROSS
180     READ EMPLOYEE$,RATE,GROSS
190 WEND
200 CLOSE #1
210 DATA "JOHN DOE",6.30,200.15
220 DATA "MARY SMITH",7.20,316.40
230 DATA "ANN JONES",5.00,80.00
240 DATA "LAST RECORD",0,0
250 END
```

Types of programs that would access such a file are the program that produces the campus phone directory, the program that provides a listing of dormitory residents to each dormitory advisor, the program that provides listings of departmental majors to each department chairperson, and so on.

Types of File Access.   There are two principal ways to access data—sequentially and directly. With the *sequential access*, the records in a file can be fetched only in the order in which they physically appear on the storage medium. A music tape provides an example of sequential access; when you play the tape, the tunes play in the order in which they are physically recorded on the tape. With *direct access*, by contrast, records can be accessed in any order. A vinyl phonograph album and a compact disk are examples; you can easily play the tunes in any order you like, and you can play them in sequential order as well.

Sequential files can only be accessed sequentially, whereas direct files can be accessed both directly and sequentially.

Creating a Sequential File.   The program shown in Figure 5-5 illustrates how to create the sequential file shown in Figure 5-6. The OPEN statement in the program indicates that the data file is to be given the name PAYFILE and stored on the disk in drive B.

You've seen most of the statements in Figure 5-5 before; however, the OPEN, WRITE, and CLOSE statements are new.

☐   *OPEN Statement.*   Every BASIC file must first be opened by an OPEN statement. The OPEN statement makes the file available for processing, sets a pointer to the beginning of the file for writing or reading records, and es-

```
"JOHN DOE",6.3,200.15
"MARY SMITH",7.2,316.4
"ANN JONES",5,80
```

Figure 5-6
The sequential file created by
the program in Figure 5-5.

tablishes a buffer in primary memory through which records are passed between the program and secondary storage.

The general format for the OPEN statement for sequential files is

```
Line # OPEN "filename" FOR ⎧OUTPUT⎫ AS # file-number
                           ⎨INPUT ⎬
                           ⎩APPEND⎭
```

The filename that you choose for your data file can be any filename that's acceptable to DOS. For example,

```
B:PAYFILE
B:PAYFILE.DAT
A:PAYFILE
C:PAYFILE
PAYFILE
PAYFILE.DAT
```

are all acceptable filenames.

In the OPEN statement's FOR clause, you must use one of the keywords OUTPUT, INPUT, or APPEND. When you are creating a file, meaning that you are writing data to it, use the word OUTPUT. When you are reading from a file, use the word INPUT. The keyword APPEND is used when you want to add records to the end of an existing file. If, for instance, there are currently 15 records in the file, APPEND will write the first record it encounters to the 16th record position in the file. Incidentally, opening a file for OUTPUT always creates a new file, so if the filename declared in the OPEN statement already exists and you want to output to it, the contents of the file will be erased and the file will be opened again as an empty file.

The file number (#1, in Figure 5-5) in the OPEN statement is used as a shorthand way to represent the filename (B:PAYFILE) in subsequent statements. You'll see this file number referenced in statements 170 and 200. If you want your program to process several files concurrently, you must use several OPEN statements and several file numbers, each of which corresponds to a particular file. For example, the statements

```
10 OPEN "B:NAMEFILE" FOR OUTPUT AS #1
20 OPEN "B:PAYFILE" FOR OUTPUT AS #2
30 OPEN "B:RATEFILE" FOR OUTPUT AS #3
```

open three files for processing.

☐ **WRITE Statement.**   The WRITE statement in line 170 is used to write data to the file. Also, it puts commas between each item (field) in each record,

Figure 5-7
A program that reads a sequential file.

```
10   REM    TITLE:   PROGRAM 5-7
20   REM
30   REM    DESCRIPTION: THIS PROGRAM READS A
40   REM       SEQUENTIAL FILE
50   REM
60   REM    AUTHOR: C.S. PARKER
70   REM    DATE: 10/5/91
80   REM
90   REM    EMPLOYEE$  = EMPLOYEE NAME
100  REM    RATE       = PAY RATE
110  REM    GROSS      = GROSS PAY
120  REM
130  REM ****************************************
140  OPEN "B:PAYFILE" FOR INPUT AS #1
150  PRINT "NAME","PAY RATE","GROSS PAY"
160  PRINT
170  WHILE NOT EOF(1)
180      INPUT #1,EMPLOYEE$,RATE,GROSS
190      PRINT EMPLOYEE$,RATE,GROSS
200  WEND
210  CLOSE #1
220  END

RUN
NAME            PAY RATE        GROSS PAY

JOHN DOE        6.3             200.15
MARY SMITH      7.2             316.4
ANN JONES       5               80
```

enabling the file to later be read by the INPUT# statement, which will be described shortly. If you are writing BASIC programs that will process several files concurrently, make sure that the file number you are referencing in the WRITE statement corresponds to the name of the file to which you want to write.

☐ *CLOSE Statement.* The CLOSE statement is used to close files. All open files must be closed before the program terminates. Also, a file must be opened before it can be closed. Once a file is closed, its file number can be assigned to another file.

Below are some acceptable forms of the CLOSE statement:

100 CLOSE #1	Closes file #1
100 CLOSE #1,#2	Closes files #1 and #2
100 CLOSE	Closes all open files

Reading a File. Once a sequential file is established in the manner just described, it can be read and processed. Before you attempt to process a file, however, you should make sure that it exists in the proper form, with commas separating data fields and each record occupying a new line. For example, if you've established PAYFILE on the B drive, as shown in Figure 5-6, get into DOS and enter

```
TYPE B:PAYFILE
```

at the A> prompt. What appears next on your screen is a listing of the contents of the file. You should inspect the file carefully before proceeding.

After you're satisfied that the file you've created does exist and is correct, it's time to develop a program to read and process it in some way. The program in Figure 5-7 reads and prints the file in Figure 5-6. The OPEN and CLOSE statements should be rather self-explanatory at this point. Files must be opened and closed when they are read just as when they are being created. Note carefully that the OPEN statement in line 140 uses the keyword INPUT, indicating that the PAYFILE is to be opened for reading.

The EOF argument in line 170 and the INPUT statement in line 180 warrant further explanation.

☐ **EOF.** In sequential file processing, EOF tests to see if the end of a file has been reached. The "1" in parentheses in line 170 means file #1; a "2" would mean file #2, and so forth. As soon as a record is read (by the INPUT statement), EOF automatically advances the file pointer to the next record.

☐ **INPUT.** In sequential file processing, the word INPUT followed by a file number has a meaning different from a conventional INPUT statement. The statement in line 180 does the reading of records for the program. It works similarly to the familiar READ statement in that, every time it is executed, the next three values from file #1 are respectively assigned to the named variables.

The programs in Figures 5-5 and 5-7 have been made very simple to enable you to focus on how file processing works. You could, if you wish, make them much more sophisticated by using subroutines, the PRINT USING statement, and the like. Virtually all of the BASIC programming tools you've encountered earlier in this *Guide* also work in a sequential file processing environment.

Solved Review Problems

Example 1

A company that produces three products currently has eight salespeople. The sales of each product by each salesperson are given in the following table:

	Units Sold		
Salesperson	Product 1	Product 2	Product 3
William Ing	100	50	65
Ed Wilson	500	0	0
Ann Johnson	200	25	600
Edna Farber	150	30	500
Norris Ames	600	80	150
Elma Jace	100	410	800
Vilmos Zisk	300	30	60
Ellen Venn	400	0	0

The latest unit prices on products 1, 2, and 3 are $1, 1.25, and .85, respectively.

Figure 5-8 A program for cross-classifying sales data.

```
10  REM     TITLE: PROGRAM 5-8
20  REM
30  REM     DESCRIPTION: THIS PROGRAM CALCULATES PRODUCT SALES
40  REM         ATTRIBUTABLE TO VARIOUS SALESPEOPLE IN A COMPANY
50  REM
60  REM     AUTHOR: C.S. PARKER
70  REM     DATE: 10/5/91
80  REM
90  REM     PERSON$     = THE SALESPERSON NAME
100 REM     NUMBER      = THE NUMBER OF SALESPEOPLE
110 REM     PRICES      = THE ARRAY OF PRODUCT PRICES
120 REM     UNITS       = THE UNITS SOLD BY A SALESPERSON
130 REM     ROWS        = THE ARRAY SAVING PRODUCT SALES
140 REM                     IN EACH ROW BEFORE THEY ARE OUTPUT
150 REM     FOOTINGS    = THE ROW TOTALS
160 REM     COLUMNS     = THE ARRAY SAVING THE COLUMN TOTALS
170 REM     GRAND       = THE GRAND TOTAL OF ALL SALES
180 REM     I,J         = LOOP VARIABLES
190 REM     A$,B$       = OUTPUT-IMAGE VARIABLES FOR PRINT USING
200 REM
210 REM     ********************************************************
220 DIM ROWS(3),COLUMNS(3),PRICES(3)
230 PRINT "   NAME        PRODUCT1   PRODUCT2   PRODUCT3      TOTAL"
240 PRINT
250 READ NUMBER
260 REM INITIALIZATIONS
270 FOR I=1 TO 3
280    COLUMNS(I) = 0
290    READ PRICES(I)
300 NEXT I
310 GRAND = 0
```

Use the preceding data to produce the following table. Use subscripted variables to represent the totals associated with the three products and the eight salespeople.

NAME	PRODUCT1	PRODUCT2	PRODUCT3	TOTAL
WILLIAM ING	100.00	62.50	55.25	217.75
ED WILSON	500.00	0.00	0.00	500.00
ANN JOHNSON	200.00	31.25	510.00	741.25
EDNA FARBER	150.00	37.50	425.00	612.50
NORRIS AMES	600.00	100.00	127.50	827.50
ELMA JACE	100.00	512.50	680.00	1,292.50
VILMOS ZISK	300.00	37.50	51.00	388.50
ELLEN VENN	400.00	0.00	0.00	400.00
TOTALS	2,350.00	781.25	1,848.75	4,980.00

Solution

A program solution to this problem is given in Figure 5-8.

Figure 5-8 *continued*

```
320 A$ = "\                \    #,###.##    #,###.##    #,###.##    #,###.##"
330 B$ = "TOTALS                #,###.##    #,###.##    #,###.##    #,###.##"
340 REM
350 REM MAIN COMPUTATIONS
360 FOR I = 1 TO NUMBER
370     FOOTINGS = 0
380     READ PERSON$
390     FOR J = 1 TO 3
400         READ UNITS
410         ROWS(J) = UNITS * PRICES(J)
420         COLUMNS(J) = COLUMNS(J) + ROWS(J)
430         FOOTINGS = FOOTINGS + ROWS(J)
440         GRAND = GRAND + ROWS(J)
450     NEXT J
460     PRINT USING A$;PERSON$,ROWS(1),ROWS(2),ROWS(3),FOOTINGS
470 NEXT I
480 PRINT
490 PRINT USING B$;COLUMNS(1),COLUMNS(2),COLUMNS(3),GRAND
500 REM ****************DATA STATEMENTS*********************
510 DATA 8
520 DATA 1,1.25,.85
530 DATA "WILLIAM ING",100,50,65
540 DATA "ED WILSON",500,0,0
550 DATA "ANN JOHNSON",200,25,600
560 DATA "EDNA FARBER",150,30,500
570 DATA "NORRIS AMES",600,80,150
580 DATA "ELMA JACE",100,410,800
590 DATA "VILMOS ZISK",300,30,60
600 DATA "ELLEN VENN",400,0,0
610 REM  **********************************************
620 END
```

The outer loop (lines 360–470) is used to read each salesperson's record. The inner loop (lines 390–450), which executes three times for every iteration of the outer loop, is used to multiply sales of each of the three products by its price, accumulate the row totals, and accumulate the column footings.

Example 2
The program in Figure 5-9 processes accounting expenses for the past month. Users of the program have several options—for example, finding the category with the greatest expense, computing total expenses (over all categories), or listing all categories with an expense exceeding $1,000. These options are presented to the user in the form of a *menu*. Once the user selects a choice on the menu, either a 1, 2, 3, or 4 is typed in, corresponding to the options in lines 310–340. Given the choice, the computer then branches to the appropriate subroutine to be processed, goes to an error-trapping routine, or ends the program. If, for example, the user selects option 2 (total cost), the computer branches to line 540 and proceeds from that point until line 620 (RETURN) is encountered. It then goes back to the main part of the program and redisplays the menu.

Figure 5-9   A menu-selection program using subroutines.
The program's output is in the inset at the bottom right.

```
10   REM     TITLE: PROGRAM 5-9
20   REM
30   REM     DESCRIPTION: THIS PROGRAM DEMONSTRATES THE
40   REM        USE OF SUBROUTINES AND MENUS
50   REM
60   REM     AUTHOR - C.S. PARKER
70   REM     DATE: 10/5/91
80   REM
90   REM     EXPENSE$    = ARRAY TO HOLD EXPENSE CATEGORIES
100  REM     AMOUNT      = ARRAY TO HOLD AMOUNTS
110  REM     RECORDS     = NUMBER OF RECORDS
120  REM     MENU        = MENU-SELECTION VARIABLE
130  REM     HOLD,HOLD$ = HOLDING VARIABLES FOR LARGEST
140  REM                        EXPENSE AND CATEGORY
150  REM     TOTAL       = TOTAL EXPENSES
160  REM
170  REM ********************************************
180  DIM EXPENSE$(100),AMOUNT(100)
190  REM
200  REM DATA ENTRY
210  READ RECORDS
220     FOR I=1 TO RECORDS
230        READ EXPENSE$(I),AMOUNT(I)
240     NEXT I
250  REM MENU AND SELECTION
260  MENU = 0
270  WHILE MENU <> 4
280     PRINT
290     PRINT "PROGRAM OPTIONS"
300     PRINT
310     PRINT "   1 - THE LARGEST CATEGORY"
320     PRINT "   2 - TOTAL COST"
330     PRINT "   3 - ALL CATEGORIES EXCEEDING $1000"
340     PRINT "   4 - END PROGRAM"
350     PRINT
360     PRINT "WHICH OPTION DO YOU WISH TO TAKE (TYPE IN NUMBER)";
370     INPUT MENU
380     IF NOT (MENU = 1 OR MENU = 2 OR MENU = 3 OR MENU = 4) THEN MENU = 5
390     ON MENU GOSUB 420,540,630,740,790
400  WEND
410     STOP
420  REM *************LARGEST COST SUBROUTINE***************
430     HOLD = AMOUNT(1)
440     HOLD$ = EXPENSE$(1)
450     FOR I=2 TO RECORDS
460        IF AMOUNT(I) <= HOLD THEN 490
470           HOLD = AMOUNT(I)
480           HOLD$ = EXPENSE$(I)
490     NEXT I
500     PRINT
510     PRINT "LARGEST EXPENSE:";HOLD$;"   (AMOUNT =";HOLD;")"
520     PRINT
530     RETURN
```

Figure 5-9 *continued*

```
540 REM *************TOTAL COST SUBROUTINE***************
550     TOTAL = 0
560     FOR I=1 TO RECORDS
570         TOTAL = TOTAL + AMOUNT(I)
580     NEXT I
590     PRINT
600     PRINT "TOTAL COST IS...$";TOTAL
610     PRINT
620     RETURN
630 REM ***********$1000-OR-MORE SUBROUTINE**************
640     PRINT
650     PRINT "CATEGORIES EXCEEDING $1000"
660     PRINT
670     PRINT "CATEGORY","EXPENSE"
680     FOR I = 1 TO RECORDS
690         IF AMOUNT(I) < 1000 THEN 710
700             PRINT EXPENSE$(I),AMOUNT(I)
710     NEXT I
720     PRINT
730     RETURN
740 REM ***********TERMINATION ROUTINE*******************
750     PRINT
760     PRINT
770     PRINT "YOU HAVE CHOSEN TO END THE PROGRAM--GOODBYE"
780     RETURN
790 REM **************ERROR ROUTINE********************
800     PRINT
810     PRINT
820     PRINT "YOU HAVE INPUT AN INCORRECT CHOICE--TRY AGAIN"
830     PRINT
840     RETURN
850 REM *************DATA STATEMENTS****************
860 DATA 8
870 DATA "SALARIES",8500,"RENT",2000,"ADVERTISING",1100
880 DATA "UTILITIES",590,"SUPPLIES",200,"DEPRECIATION",1200
890 DATA "INSURANCE",300,"TAXES",150
900 REM ********************************************
910 END
```

```
        PROGRAM OPTIONS

            1 - THE LARGEST CATEGORY
            2 - TOTAL COST
            3 - ALL CATEGORIES EXCEEDING $1000
            4 - END PROGRAM

        WHICH OPTION DO YOU WISH TO TAKE (TYPE IN NUMBER)?2

        CATEGORIES EXCEEDING $1000

        CATEGORY        EXPENSE
        SALARIES        8500
        RENT            2000
        ADVERTISING     1100
        DEPRECIATION    1200

        NEXT MENU SELECTION (TYPE IN NUMBER)?
```

Exercises

Instructions: Provide an answer to each of the following questions.

1. Consider the following program:

    ```
    10 DIM A(5)
    20 FOR I=1 TO 5
    30 READ A(I)
    40 LET A(I)=A(I)+1
    50 NEXT I
    60 DATA 35,18,-6,42,27
    ```

    What is the final value of

    a. A(1)?   b. A(2)?   c. A(3)?   d. A(4)?   e. A(5)?

2. Consider the following program:

    ```
    10 DIM A(6)
    20 A(1)=0
    30 FOR I=2 TO 6
    40 READ A(I)
    50 LET A(I)=A(I-1)
    60 NEXT I
    70 DATA 35,18,-6,42,27
    ```

    What is the final value of

    a. A(1)?   b. A(2)?   c. A(3)?   d. A(4)?   e. A(5)?

3. Consider the following program:

    ```
    10 DIM A(4,4)
    20 FOR I=1 TO 4
    30 FOR J=1 TO 4
    40 READ A(I,J)
    50 NEXT J
    60 NEXT I
    70 DATA 12,2,0,3,1,4,2,7,6,10,9,0,11,3,8,7
    ```

    What is the final value of

    a. A(1,3)?   b. A(2,2)?   c. A(3,4)?   d. A(4,3)?

4. What does the following program do?

    ```
    10 DIM A(20), B(20)
    20 FOR I=1 TO 5
    30 READ A(I), B(I)
    40 A(I)=A(I)-B(I)
    50 NEXT I
    60 DATA 6,8,4,5,7,1,0,2,8,3
    ```

5. What are the values of all variables in the C array when the following program has finished executing?

```
10 S=0
20 FOR J=1 TO 5
30 READ A(J)
40 S=S+A(J)
50 NEXT J
60 FOR I=1 TO 5
70 C(I+1)=S-A(I)
80 NEXT I
90 DATA 10,4,1,6,8
```

Programming Problems

Instructions: Write a BASIC program to do each of the following tasks.

1. The following is a list of salaries of the six employees in a certain company:

Name	Salary
T. Agasi	$43,000
F. Smith	$31,000
K. Johnston	$22,000
P. Miner	$18,000
C. Altman	$27,000
A. Lu	$19,000

   Calculate and output the average salary for the company as well as the names of all people whose salaries exceed the average.

2. Read the 10 numbers in the following list, and then output the list in reverse order (that is, 12, 43, 6, etc.):

   31, 15, 85, 36, 22, 81, 70, 6, 43, 12

3. The following list contains names and sexes of people at XYZ Company: Janice Racza (female), Bill Smith (male), Debra Parks (female), Chantelle Johnson (female), William Anderson (male), Art James (male), Bill Finley (male), and Ellen Woo (female).

   Read the list into the computer in the order given. Then prepare and output two separate lists—one composed of all of the males and the other composed of all of the females.

4. Write a program that reads the following matrix,

$$\begin{bmatrix} 8 & 7 & 3 \\ 2 & 4 & 1 \\ 6 & 5 & 8 \end{bmatrix}$$

   adds the number 5 to each element (number) of the matrix, and prints the result.

5. Refer to Programming Problem 7 on page 31 of the *Guide*. Write a program to enter the five student records into a file. Then write another program to produce student bills in the manner described in the problem statement.

Appendix 1: BASIC Statement Commands

Statement	Description	Example
DEF	Sets up a user-defined function (80)	`90 DEF` `   FNC(S1,S2)=.15*S1+.10*S2`
DIM	Dimensions an array (73)	`120 DIM X(12)`
END	The last statement in a program (24)	`250 END`

FOR/NEXT	The beginning and ending statements in a loop (47)	`160 FOR I=1 TO N`
		`      .`
		`      .`
		`      .`
		`190 NEXT I`

GOSUB/ RETURN	Branch to a subroutine; Return to main program from subroutine (51)	`120 GOSUB 150`
		`      .`
		`      .`
		`      .`
		`190 RETURN`

IF/THEN	A conditional branch (21)	`110 IF A=-1 THEN 160`
IF/THEN/ELSE	A conditional branch (21)	`110 IF S>5000 THEN B=500` `                ELSE B=0`
INPUT	Enables data to be entered interactively (45)	`80 INPUT X`
LET	An assignment (replacement) statement (19)	`30 LET C=A+B`
ON . . . GOSUB	Branches to a specific case (52)	`100 ON M GOSUB 300,400,500`
PRINT	Displays or prints program output (20)	`160 PRINT N$`

PRINT USING	Enables neatly formatted output (62)	`100 A$="###.##"`
		`      .`
		`      .`
		`      .`
		`200 PRINT USING A$;X`

READ/DATA	Assigns values to variables from a list of data (19)	`20 READ A,B`
		`      .`
		`      .`
		`      .`
		`50 DATA 8,16`

REM	A program remark (23)	`100 REM THIS IS A REMARK`
STOP	Stops a program (45)	`80 STOP`

WHILE/WEND	The beginning and ending statements in a loop (21)	`150 WHILE X>0`
		`      .`
		`      .`
		`      .`
		`200 WEND`

Note: Numbers in parentheses in the second column are the pages on which the statement is described.

Appendix 2: Reserved Words

ABS	DELETE	INT	OPEN	SOUND
AND	DIM	INTER$	OPTION	SPACE$
ASC	DRAW	IOCTL	OR	SCP
ATN	EDIT	IOCTL$	OUT	SQR
AUTO	ELSE	KEY	PAINT	STEP
BEEP	END	KILL	PEEK	STICK
BLOAD	ENVIRON	LEFT$	PEN	STOP
BSAVE	ENVIRON$	LEN	PLAY	STR$
CALL	EOF	LET	PMAP	SRIG
CDBL	EQV	LINE	POINT	STRING$
CHAIN	ERASE	LIST	POKE	SWAP
CHDIR	ERDEV	LLIST	POS	SYSTEM
CHR$	ERDEV$	LOAD	PRESET	TAB
CINT	ERL	LOC	PRINT	TAN
CIRCLE	ERR	LOCATE	PRINT#	THEN
CLEAR	ERROR	LOF	PSET	TIME$
CLOSE	EXP	LOG	PUT	TO
CLS	FIELD	LPOS	RANDOMIZE	TROFF
COLOR	FILES	LPRINT	READ	TRON
COM	FIX	LSET	REM	USING
COMMON	FNxxx	MERGE	RENUM	USR
CONT	FOR	MID$	RESET	VAL
COS	FRE	MKDIR	RESTORE	VARPTR
CSNG	GET	MKD$	RESUME	VARPTR$
CSRLIN	GOSUB	MKI$	RETURN	WAIT
CVD	GOTO	MKS$	RIGHT$	WEND
CVI	HEX$	MOD	RMDIR	WHILE
CVS	IF	MOTOR	RND	WIDTH
DATA	IMP	NAME	RSET	WINDOW
DATE$	INKEY$	NEW	RUN	WRITE
DEF	INP	NEXT	SAVE	WRITE#
DEFDBL	INPUT	NOT	SCREEN	XOR
DEFINT	INPUT#	OCT$	SGN	
DEFSNG	INPUT$	OFF	SHELL	
DEFSTR	INSTR	ON	SIN	